japanese
INSPIRATIONS

japanese
inspirations

18 Quilted Projects

JANET HAIGH

Martingale
& COMPANY

For Fusako Kubo and Atsuko Morimoto and in memory of Janet Arnold

FIRST PUBLISHED IN GREAT BRITAIN IN 2000
by Collins & Brown Limited
The Chrysalis Building
Bramley Road
London
W10 6SP

Editorial Director: Sarah Hoggett
Editor: Catherine Ward
Designer: Debbie Mole
Photography: John Heseltine

That Patchwork Place is an imprint of Martingale & Company.

Martingale & Company
20205 144th Avenue NE
Woodinville, WA 98072-8478 USA
www.martingale-pub.com

Reproduction by Global Colour, Malaysia
Printed and bound in Singapore by Imago Ltd

05 04   6 5 4

ISBN 1-56477-323-X

Library of Congress Cataloging-in-Publication Data Is Available.

MISSION STATEMENT
We are dedicated to providing quality
products and service by working
together to inspire creativity and to
enrich the lives we touch.

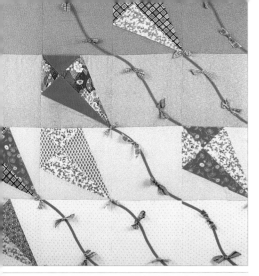

contents

Introduction

My fascination for Oriental textiles, Japanese designs in particular, inspired this book and began at an

early age. I have tried to capture the unique style of the prints, embroideries, and weavings of the Orient

by combining Western and Japanese techniques in the following patchwork and appliqué projects.

あけまして
おめでとう
ございます

昭和六十二年元旦

ABOVE: **Dressed for a celebration** *Miwa, aged 3, wears a brilliant red patterned kimono with matching hat and handbag.*

RIGHT: **Oriental colors** *Rows of toys from a street vendor's stall and a detail of my Chinese jacket with the delicate flowers stitched in the shaded tones typical of all Oriental embroidery.*

ONE OF MY BROTHERS WAS A merchant seaman. He traveled extensively in the Far East, disappearing for months at a time and returning with delicate hand-painted china tea services, exotic brocade dressing gowns, and elegant fans for my mother and his wife. For me he brought strange toys, games, kites, and brilliantly patterned and colored fans. I also remember wonderful Chinese paper lanterns that decorated our Christmas trees for years and paper garlands hung with silk tassels and curious emblems that I later realized were charms sold at shrines to attract wealth or good luck at the new year. As a young child I had played dressing-up with Chinese *cheong-sams*, embroidered shawls with long silk tassels, and kimonos that were brought for my mother by her brother when he had also been a sailor as a young man.

I can remember the first kimono that I bought, a small red, purple, and green print silk robe with simple flowers and shady cloud designs. I purchased it from an English antique shop and used it as a dressing gown. I was fascinated by the printed design and started to search out information about it. I discovered that this particular robe was designed to be worn by a young unmarried girl, as the predominant color was red, and that it was a winter design of plum blossoms and pine needles.

Intrigued, I started to visit shops that imported secondhand kimonos. The robes were old and worn, but I was entranced by the beautiful linear drawing of the printed patterns and the subtle colors

ABOVE: **Childhood inspiration** *Toys, candy wrappers, hashi (Japanese chopsticks), silk-covered shell ornaments, a costume doll in traditional kimono, and Japanese folding and Chinese flat fans are all reminiscent of my childhood and the presents brought back by my seafaring brother.*

LEFT: **Children's masks** *Rows of masks ranging from traditional folk heroes to cartoon characters.*

毛金
本金
embroidery thread (gold)

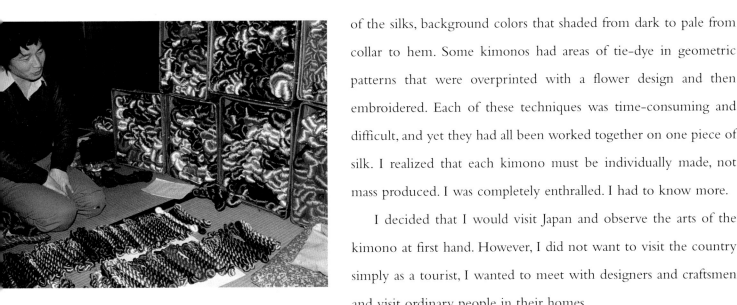

of the silks, background colors that shaded from dark to pale from collar to hem. Some kimonos had areas of tie-dye in geometric patterns that were overprinted with a flower design and then embroidered. Each of these techniques was time-consuming and difficult, and yet they had all been worked together on one piece of silk. I realized that each kimono must be individually made, not mass produced. I was completely enthralled. I had to know more.

I decided that I would visit Japan and observe the arts of the kimono at first hand. However, I did not want to visit the country simply as a tourist, I wanted to meet with designers and craftsmen and visit ordinary people in their homes.

LEFT & ABOVE:
Japanese experiences
Photographs and mementos from my visit include scenes from a secondhand kimono stall in a Kyoto market, the silk merchant where I bought the brilliantly dyed skeins, cups of dye in the kimono designer's studio, and a Kabuki poster featuring actors in traditional makeup. The inset circle is a detail of my first kimono.

RIGHT: **Sketch book** *Blue and white woven braids, indigo shibori or tie-dye, and stenciled cotton samples surround a page of stencils stippled into my sketch book by a kimono designer.*

After much inquiry, the English costume archivist Janet Arnold gave me an introduction to Fusako Kubo, the costume historian of the court robes of the Japanese Imperial family and lecturer and writer on kimono design. Her daughter, Atsuko Morimoto, invited me to stay with her family in Osaka, initially for a week. From Osaka it was easy to travel on the train to Kyoto, where the traditional textile designers and craftspeople worked.

Best of all, Mrs. Kubo knew these craftspeople personally. She arranged for me to meet silk dyers and weavers, indigo stencil printers, kimono designers, and embroiderers, while her husband patiently escorted me to temples, gardens, museums, and palaces. I saw the kimonos of the nobility and the No theater, rich silks woven and printed with silver and gold, intricately woven *obi*, and braids that wrap around and tie the layered garments. I was invited into family homes and gardens, given traditional meals and, most memorably, taken cherry blossom viewing by Mr. Morimoto and his young daughter Kyoko.

I studied as much as I could about the textiles that I had seen. I was taught to ply silks and cut stencils, and given recipes for dyes and rice-paste resists for silk painting. I soaked in all that I could manage in the five weeks that I eventually stayed with the family, for I had contracted to have an embroidery exhibition in a London gallery on my return.

I decided that the exhibition embroideries would contain all the new techniques that I had seen. I conveniently forgot that all the Japanese craftsmen and women had undergone at least a seven-year apprenticeship and that they only practiced one craft.

I began my experimenting with the materials that I had brought back from Japan. I eventually managed to make small areas of each technique, a bit of blended dyed silk, a portion of couched gold embroidery, a minute piece of tie-dyeing, but trying to put all the techniques together on one piece of silk cloth defeated me. Finally I devised a system of appliquéing all the bits together so that the resulting work appeared to be made from one piece of fabric.

LEFT: **Banners**
I embroidered these carp banners for a group of brothers for Boy's Festival day. The carp who swims against the current is seen as a symbol of strength and vigor.

BELOW: **Embroidery**
My silk embroidery made in memory of cherry blossom viewing in Kyoto.

Recently, looking afresh at books of kimono design, I realized how similar the geometric designs are to Western patchwork. The woven hexagonal and triangular backgrounds of Japanese designs are the same as traditional patchwork. What makes the kimono designs different is in the placing of various patterns together and the addition of freer, more rhythmical motifs on the geometric surface.

Stencil and appliqué techniques are also common to both traditions. I experimented with fusible web to make gilding fabric very easy, and found that simple dip-dyeing can be mastered by children. When all or just one of these techniques is added to traditional patchwork, the designs look distinctly Oriental.

In the following pages I have devised designs that use both European and Japanese techniques. You can sample a small piece of embroidery, stenciling, or gilding and then incorporate it in a more familiar patchwork design, or you can combine traditional patchwork patterns in Japanese combinations. As you gain more confidence in sampling decorative techniques, you will develop your own ideas and designs.

LEFT: **Metallic threads** *Gold and silver threads were couched and blended with silks in the first embroidery I made after returning from Japan. I copied the techniques from a Japanese embroidery book by following the pictures.*

BELOW: **Cranes** *The inset circle shows gold and silver machine-embroidered cranes flying across a wedding kimono.*

ABOVE: **Golds and silvers** *This No theater mask, the ko-omote, is for the character of a sweet young girl. It lies on gold and silver woven fabrics for the obi and obi-jime, the traditional wide sash and braids that wrap and secure the kimono when worn by women. These are typical of the rich fabrics that are used for theatrical robes. Papers can also be gilded for wrappers and fans.*

Japanese-style fabrics

Some Oriental fabrics are easily available and recognizable, but the range is much wider than most

people realize. Where authentic fabrics are not easily found, the following pages will be invaluable to

help source Western fabrics and to transform plain cloth using simple Japanese techniques.

Weaves

The rich, glamorous metallic and silk woven fabrics that are used for the obi (traditional wide sash worn with a kimono) and the costumes of the No and Kabuki theaters are difficult to find outside Japan. However, smaller-scale evening-wear fabrics often have Oriental patterns, usually Chinese in design, and are readily available. Necktie brocades are also perfect because of their rich colorings. The heavier woven stripes and plaids found in upholstery fabrics have both the color and character of the handsome silk theatrical fabrics.

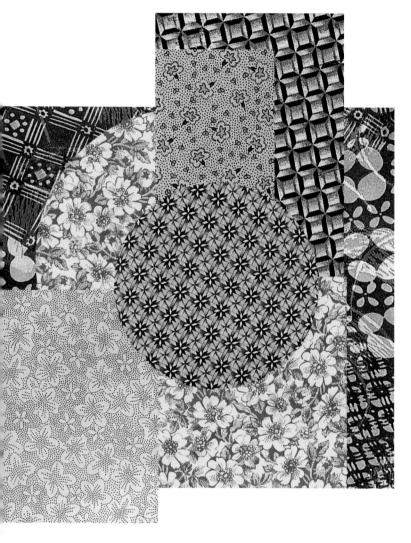

Background Prints

The simple one or two color geometric prints, regularly used for patchwork, look remarkably like the komon *or small-scale stencil resist prints used for informal kimonos. Originally worn by men – in somber colors like indigo blue, grays, browns, and dull purples – printed onto ramie or cotton, the tiny patterns are now easily found in all colors and are very useful for providing interesting backgrounds for larger designs.*

Tie-dyes

Known in the West as Ikat, *the warp threads of the fabric are pattern dyed before weaving, resulting in hazy patterns when the weft threads are woven across them.*

These patterned fabrics are widely available both in silk and cotton for furnishings as well as for fine woven scarves. In Japan, indigo-dyed cottons in simple stripes are popular for summer kimonos, as are the more refined striped silks. It should be relatively easy to find similar types of fabrics.

Kimono Prints

The typical silk prints that we associate with kimono design were traditionally painted in a time-consuming technique, yusen, *which made idealized pictures of Japanese life. Flowers, butterflies, birds, and animals are set against rich and varied geometric patterns and motifs of fans, kites, waves, clouds, and snowflakes. The stylized designs make beautiful, exquisitely drawn and colored fabrics. Look for the same subject matter, but on a smaller scale than the originals, and try to find designs that are crisply drawn.*

Creating Japanese patterns

The richness of Japanese fabrics is due to the way that several techniques are combined to make up

one design. By using traditional Western patchwork patterns in different combinations, or by adding

Japanese motifs and shapes, familiar patchwork can be given an Oriental flavor.

Checkerboard

The system of alternating light and dark colors, print and solid (plain) squares, or even contrasting print squares, results in the type of bold fabrics that are often used for Japanese theatrical costumes.

The simple green and purple silk checkerboard relies on two strong contrasting colors. The richness comes from the subtly different textures and tones of the fabrics. The striped diamonds are formed from squares made of two contrasting striped triangles sewn together. Rotating the squares permits variations of this pattern to be made.

Diagonal

The strong diagonal design is constant in much Japanese patterning; it is seen dividing plates, screens, and even kimonos. The two sides need to be carefully balanced over large areas. The pale silvery colors of the metallic fabrics and silks help to blend the different geometric designs with the random circles of the motifs.

However, on the smaller scale of a cushion, the design elements can be much more varied. Here, two equally rich patterns have been married together; the dark background squares are balanced by the light triangles.

Bands

Bands, whether vertical or horizontal, are the simplest of all patterns. The possibilities are endless, and many different patterns are often striped together on traditional kimono designs.

The dazzling blue and white stars below are interspersed with a band of hexagons to create a pattern of stars and stripes. More complex and subtle bands are made from hand-pieced sections, and many of the simpler patchwork patterns could be layered one on top of the other in boundless variation to make subtle and unusual designs. The wave pattern depends on repeating stripes to give the appearance of the sea.

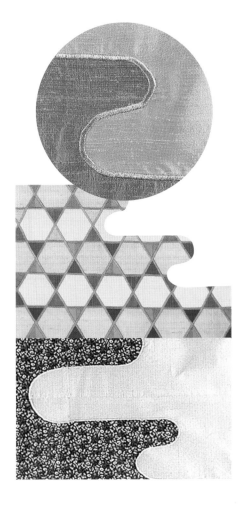

Clouds

The most characteristic of all the systems of combining patterns, this undulating line will make any combination of fabrics look immediately Oriental.

The simplest way to achieve the join is to appliqué one cloudy shape onto another by machine stitching. Here, two coordinating silks have been joined with gold metallic thread in a close zigzag stitch. Interestingly, gold is a very useful neutral thread for combining colors and its use is authentic Oriental practice. A cloud effect can be strengthened by careful use of color, and a blue and white contrast immediately evokes the sky. Pieces of patchwork can be used as cloud shapes if care is exercised in cutting and stitching.

Crazy

Crazy patchwork gained popularity when Japanese designs were introduced to the West toward the end of the nineteenth century. The haphazard effects were thought to resemble the asymmetric Japanese designs.

When creating crazy patchwork; be careful with the colors. Here, earthy colors have been used with some somber, dark patterns and a lighter neutral to give cohesion to the design. A useful guide is to use three or four shades of the same color throughout the patchwork.

The inclusion of the stars makes for strong contrasts that need careful balancing. Different colors and stitches can be used when embroidering over the seams to help balance the design.

Placing motifs

The placing of one motif onto a patterned background and maintaining a balanced design is the quintessential art of Japanese textiles.

The appliquéd shapes need to be very strong, and shapes such as circles, fans, and diamonds are all good for this purpose.

The softer embroidered motifs need a sympathetic and regular background of colors and shapes. The curved fan is always an interesting motif against a geometric ground.

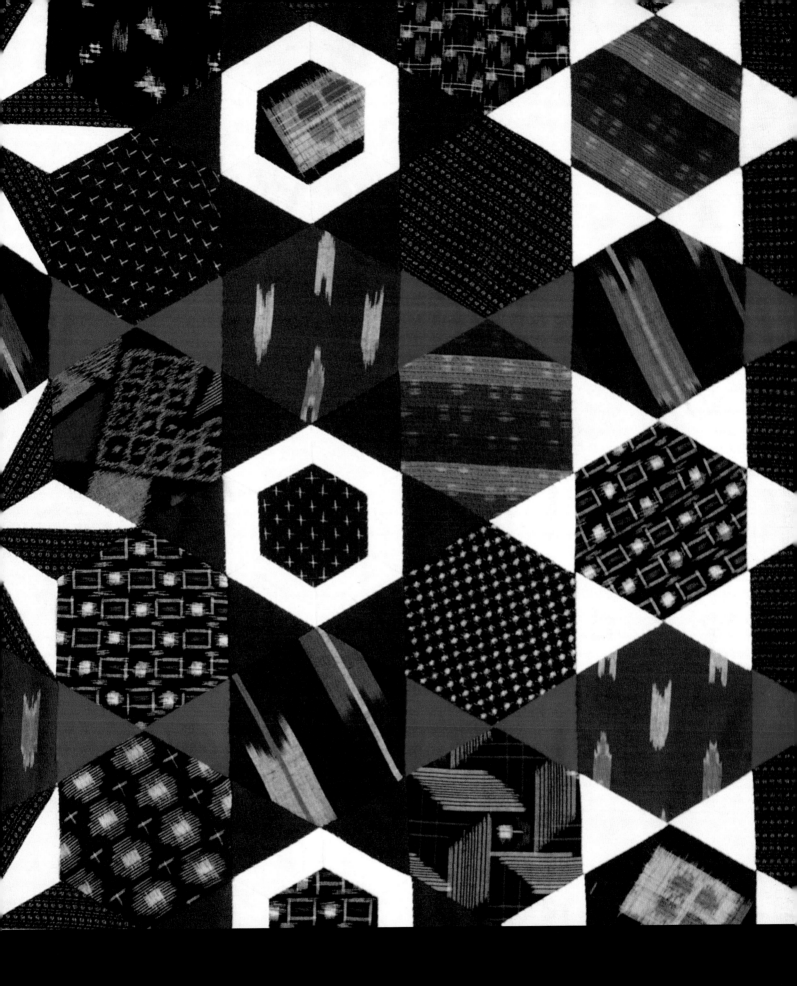

patchwork techniques

Hand Piecing

MANY TRADITIONAL PATCHWORK SHAPES with precise corners or angles, such as hexagons and diamonds, are difficult to stitch by machine and are more accurate to work by hand. The most precise method of joining complex shapes such as hexagons and diamonds is to mount them on backing papers (see opposite) before whipstitching the shapes together by hand. Although this method is time-consuming, hand piecing is a very satisfying method of assembly which gives exemplary results – especially when piecing "fancy" fabrics such as silks, satins, or brocades.

In this section of the book, I have included instructions for cutting out and preparing the fabrics, mounting them on backing papers, and assembling them into both simple and complex patterns. The patchwork blocks that result

can either be used in their own right to form the basis of a project, or they can form intricate backgrounds for applied decoration such as hand embroidery, stenciling, or appliqué (see pages 36–41). Among the hand-pieced designs featured here are traditional star motifs, such as the Hexagon and Compass star, and popular Japanese variations such as the Tortoiseshell star. Another authentic Japanese pattern is the pinebark motif, which is made by joining sets of diamond shapes together by hand to produce a pattern that is thought to resemble the bark of the pine cone (see above center).

CUTTING BACKING PAPERS

When fabric patches are pieced by hand, it is useful to mount them on paper templates for support during assembly. These can be removed after the patchwork is complete. Backing papers are always cut to the finished size of the patch, with no seam allowances added.

1 Trace the relevant template (with no seam allowances added) onto tracing paper and cut out the shape carefully using scissors.

2 Draw around the shape onto stiff cardboard. Lay the cardboard on a cutting mat and cut out the template with a sharp craft knife.

3 Place the cardboard template on scrap paper, draw around it, and cut out the shape. (You will need one backing paper for every fabric patch.)

CUTTING AND PREPARING FABRIC PATCHES

The backing papers are used as templates during cutting to insure that every fabric patch is cut to the same size. This method is ideal for cutting patches with precise corners and angles.

1 Place a backing paper on the wrong side of the fabric and pin down, leaving a 5 mm (¹/₄ in) seam allowance all around. Use a pencil or tailor's chalk and a ruler to mark the seam allowances on the fabric and cut out the shape. Don't worry if the seam allowances are not strictly accurate, since the backing papers will be left in position as a guide during assembly.

2 With a backing paper pinned to the wrong side of the fabric patch, fold the seam allowances over the paper and baste down on the reverse with contrasting thread. For best results, knot the thread on the right side of the fabric for easy removal of the threads and papers later. Mount the remaining patches on backing papers in the same way.

3 Arrange the patches in your chosen order on a flat surface, ready for piecing. Hold two patches right sides together and make sure the corners are even. Whipstitch the edges together, taking care not to catch the backing papers in your line of stitching. Join the remaining patches in the same manner. Leave all the backing papers in place until after the patchwork is finished.

TRIANGLE STAR

This Triangle Star is made up of twelve equilateral triangles – three in solid (plain) fabric and nine in contrasting pattern – which are joined to form a star shape.

A completed Triangle Star.

1 Trace the triangle template from page 102 and cut the required number of backing papers with no seam allowances added. For each Triangle Star you will need 12 backing papers.

2 Pin the backing papers to your chosen fabrics, mark 5 mm (¹/₄ in) seam allowances, and cut out three triangles in solid (plain) fabric and nine in striped fabric on the marked lines.

3 With the backing papers pinned to the wrong side of the fabric, fold the seam allowances over the papers and baste down on the reverse using contrasting thread.

4 Arrange the patches in your chosen order, making sure that contrasting fabrics are correctly coordinated. Hold two patches right sides together and make sure the corners are level. Whipstitch the edges together, taking care not to catch the backing papers in your line of stitching. Join the remaining patches to complete the star pattern.

> **The Triangle Star features in the Katsuri Star Throw (pp. 54–7) and the Three Friends Screen (pp. 98–9).**

HEXAGON STAR

For this design, six triangles are pieced around a central hexagon patch to form a star shape. The pattern works well with solid (plain) and print fabrics in contrasting colors.

A completed Hexagon Star.

1 Trace the two templates from page 120 and use to cut the required number of backing papers with no seam allowances added. For each star you will need one hexagonal and six triangular papers.

2 Pin the backing papers to your chosen fabrics, mark 5 mm (¹/₄ in) seam allowances, and cut out the fabric patches on the marked lines.

3 With the backing papers pinned to the wrong side of the fabric, fold the seam allowances over the papers and baste down on the reverse using contrasting thread.

4 Arrange the triangles around the central hexagon, ready for piecing together. Align one edge of one triangle to one edge of the hexagon, right sides together. Whipstitch the edges together, taking care not to catch the backing papers in your line of stitching. Join the remaining triangles around the central hexagon to complete the star.

> **The Hexagon Star features in the Katsuri Star Throw (pp. 54–7) and the Three Friends Screen (pp. 98–9).**

TORTOISESHELL STAR

This double hexagon star is made in the same way as the single Hexagon Star (left), but it also includes a band of cream quadrilaterals around the central hexagon. Notice how each shape is a different color fabric.

A completed Tortoiseshell Star.

1 Trace the three templates from page 102 and cut the required number of backing papers with no seam allowances added. For each Tortoiseshell Star you will need one hexagonal, six quadrilateral, and six triangular backing papers.

2 Pin the backing papers to the fabric, mark 5 mm ($^1/_4$ in) seam allowances, and cut out the fabric patches on the marked lines.

3 With the backing papers pinned to the wrong side of the fabric patches, fold the seam allowances over the papers and baste down on the reverse using contrasting thread.

4 Arrange the patches in your chosen order, ready for piecing together. Align one edge of the hexagon with one edge of a quadrilateral, right sides together, and whipstitch the edges together. Join the remaining quadrilaterals around the central hexagon to form a double hexagon. Then piece the triangles around the outside to complete the star pattern.

The Tortoiseshell Star features in the Katsuri Star Throw (pp. 54–7) and the Three Friends Screen (pp. 98–9).

COMPASS STAR

The Compass Star comprises twelve isosceles triangles, which are pieced together in pairs along their long sides before being joined into a star shape.

A completed Compass Star.

1 Trace the triangle template from page 102 and cut the required number of backing papers with no seam allowances added. For each Compass Star you will need twelve triangular backing papers.

2 Pin the backing papers to the fabric, mark 5 mm ($^1/_4$ in) seam allowances and cut out six fabric patches in solid (plain) fabric and six in striped fabric on the marked lines.

3 With the backing papers pinned to the wrong side of the fabric patches, fold the seam allowances over the papers and baste down on the reverse using contrasting thread.

4 Hold two contrasting patches right sides together and make sure that the corners are even. Whipstitch the patches together along one long edge only, making sure you do not catch the backing papers in your line of stitching. Join the remaining patches in pairs in the same way. Finally, join the resulting pieced diamonds to complete the star.

The Compass Star features in the Katsuri Star Throw (pp. 54–7) and the Three Friends Screen (pp. 98–9).

COMBINING MACHINE AND HAND PATCHWORK

THE MOST EFFECTIVE way to combine two different patchwork pieces is to use a strong diagonal line cutting across a square. The best way to do this is to use two equally sized patchwork triangles, worked by hand, machine, or a combination of both as shown here. Given this treatment, the simplest of patchwork strips, checks, and triangles can look stunning when teamed with another piece of patchwork.

It is important to consider the balance of color when combining patchwork. If the overall tones are similar, then it is easier to make the different scales and patterns work together. Here, the samples have all been taken from the Fall projects to make sure that the colors blend together easily. These combinations of patchwork from different projects work very well together and could be used to make attractive cushion covers.

Experiment by making different pieces of triangular-shaped patchwork with coordinating fabrics and then trying one against the other. You will find that you can create all kinds of new and different designs in this way.

TRIANGLE STRIP

This pattern is made up from right-angled triangles.
The design looks strongest when solid (plain) and print fabrics are alternated
in two contrasting colors.

A strip of hand-pieced triangles.

1 Trace the triangle template from page 102 and use to cut the required number of backing papers with no seam allowances added.

2 Pin the backing papers to your chosen fabrics, mark 5 mm (¼ in) seam allowances on the fabric, and cut out the patches on the marked lines.

3 With the backing papers pinned to the wrong side of the fabric patches, fold the seam allowances over the papers and baste down on the reverse.

4 Join some of the solid (plain) and print triangles in pairs by whipstitching along one edge only.

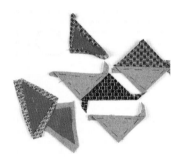

5 Arrange the resulting pieced and plain shapes in your chosen order, ready for assembly. Whipstitch the shapes together to complete the block. Here three pieced squares – made by joining pairs of triangles along their long edges – are being assembled into a strip with individual triangles set around the sides.

The hand-pieced triangle features in the Cloudy Fan Cushion (pp.76–7) and the Three Friends Screen (pp.98–9).

PINEBARK PATTERN

Each pinebark unit contains four diamond shapes in the same
color or in shades of one color. Here three pinebark units in alternating fabrics
. have been joined.

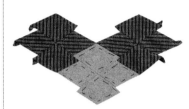

Pinebark units combined.

4 Fold the seam allowances over the papers and baste down on the reverse.

1 Trace the diamond templates from page 102 and cut the required number of backing papers with no seam allowances added. For each pinebark unit you will need two backing papers of template A and two of template B.

2 Pin the backing papers to the fabric, mark 5 mm (¼ in) seam allowances, and cut out four fabric patches in each color on the marked lines.

3 Carefully pin a backing paper to the wrong side of every fabric patch, ready for assembly.

The Pinebark pattern features in the Tortoiseshell Cushion (pp.92–3).

5 Hold two patches right sides together, making sure that one corner is even, and whipstitch along one side only. Join the remaining patches in pairs in the same way, then join the pairs to complete the unit.

6 Join the resulting units to form a strip.

Machine Piecing

WHEN LARGE AREAS OF PATCHWORK are required, it is often preferable to sew the pieces together by machine. This method of assembly can result in a uniform-looking piece, and machine-sewn patchwork provides a very stable ground on which to apply other surface decorations such as appliqué or embroidery. Bear in mind, however, that although machine stitching is faster than hand stitching, this method requires care and attention in the early stages. Every piece must be cut out and marked with very accurate seam allowances. While most simple shapes lend themselves to machine piecing, those with precise angles or corners such as hexagons or diamond shapes are much more easily and accurately stitched by hand (see pages 18–21).

In this section of the book, I have included instructions for both cutting and assembly. Among the machine-pieced designs featured here are simple but traditional patterns incorporating squares such as the Checkerboard (bottom left) and Diamond (top left) block and those composed of triangles, including the Pinwheel and Sharkstooth block. The patchwork that results can either be used on its own or combined with other forms of decoration – for example, the squares with appliquéd motifs in the Noble Medallion Throw (above center). The patchwork can also be used as a strong background for an embroidered motif, such as in the Tree Peony Cushion (page 64).

CUTTING TEMPLATES

Templates for machine patchwork should always be cut with seam allowances added. Precision is vital when cutting templates, and it helps to transfer all markings – including grain lines – onto the card template, since a small discrepancy at this stage will be magnified later.

1 Carefully trace the relevant templates from the back of the book onto tracing paper. Make sure that you transfer all seam allowances and grain lines, although experienced quilters may not need to mark seam allowances. Cut out the shapes with a sharp pair of scissors.

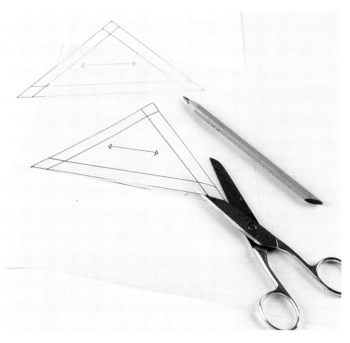

2 Turn the tracing paper over and place it on a piece of stiff cardboard. Draw around the shape with a sharp pencil, then transfer the marks by going over the outlines with a soft pencil or copying them directly onto the cardboard. Place the cardboard on a cutting mat and cut out the shape with a craft knife.

3 Use a pair of sharp scissors to cut small notches into the seam allowances along each edge, as shown. These markings can be transferred onto the fabric with a pencil or tailor's chalk and used as a guide when pinning and stitching the patches together (see right). (Experienced quilters may find notching unnecessary.)

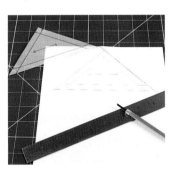

CHECKERBOARD BLOCK

This Checkerboard block is made up of sixteen squares – eight in small, all-over prints and eight in large, contrasting prints. Notice how the seams in each row of squares align exactly with the seams in the rows above and below them.

A completed Checkerboard block.

1 Trace the square template (see page 103), including the marked seam allowance, and make a cardboard template. Use your template to mark the required number of squares on your chosen fabrics – this block consists of sixteen square patches. Mark the notched seam allowances in each corner of every patch with a soft pencil or tailor's chalk. (Experienced quilters may find notching unnecessary.) Cut out the shapes individually.

The Checkerboard block features in the Spring Fans Screen (pp. 50–3) and the Noble Medallion Throw (pp.82–5).

2 Pin two contrasting patches right sides together along one edge, using a 1 cm (⅜ in) seam allowance. Machine stitch together. Press the seams to one side on the reverse for light fabrics and flat open on the reverse for heavy fabrics. Join the remaining patches in pairs in the same manner.

3 Join two sets of pairs to form a row of four patches, alternating colors as shown. Press the seams to one side on the reverse for light fabrics and open on the reverse for heavy fabrics. Make three more rows in the same manner. Pin the four rows together in the correct order, aligning seams carefully. Then machine stitch the rows together to complete the Checkerboard block. Press all seams open on the reverse.

DIAMOND BLOCK

This contains seven rows of patches, which are joined and set on point.
The resulting 25-patch block can be trimmed at the sides
to form a square if necessary.

A completed Diamond block.

1 Trace the square template (see page 103), including the marked seam allowance, and use to mark the required number of squares on your fabrics. Cut out the squares. For this block you will need sixteen of fabric A, three of fabric B, three of fabric C, and three of fabric D.

2 Join the patches to form seven rows, using a 1 cm (⅜ in) seam allowance, and alternating the fabrics as shown. Rows 1 and 7 contain a single patch of fabric A. Row 2 contains three patches, arranged A, B, A. Row 3 has five patches, arranged A, C, A, B, A. Row 4 contains seven patches, arranged A, D, A, C, A, B, A. Row 5 contains five patches, arranged A, D, A, C, A. Row 6 contains three patches,

arranged A, D, A. Press the seams on each row to one side for light fabrics and open for heavy fabrics.

3 Join the rows, aligning seams carefully.

4 Trim the sides to form a square block.

The Diamond block features in the Noble Medallion Throw (pp. 82–5), the Mist and Snow Bedcover (pp.94–7), and the Three Friends Screen (pp.98–9).

SHARKSTOOTH BLOCK

This pattern is made from equilateral triangles in alternating colors,
which are joined in rows. The resulting block can be trimmed to form a
square if necessary.

A completed Sharkstooth block.

1 Trace the template from page 104 and make a cardboard template, including the marked seam allowance (see page 25). Use the template to mark the required number of triangles on your chosen fabrics. For this block you will need fourteen of fabric A, three of fabric B, four of fabric C, three of fabric D, and four of fabric E. Mark the notched seam allowances in each corner of every patch with a soft pencil or tailor's chalk. (Experienced quilters may find notching unnecessary.)

2 Cut out the patches with a sharp pair of scissors.

3 Join the patches to form four rows, using a 1 cm (⅜ in) seam allowance, alternating solid (plain) and print fabrics as shown (see left). Press the seams to one side for light fabrics and press open for heavy fabrics.

4 Baste the four rows together in the correct order, matching seams carefully.

5 Machine stitch over the basted lines to complete the block. Press on the reverse.

The Sharkstooth block features in the Noble Medallion Throw (pp.82–5) and the Three Friends Screen (pp.98–9).

COMBINING PATCHWORK AND APPLIQUÉ

IT IS SIMPLE TO RECREATE the rich and varied character of Japanese textiles in patchwork and appliqué designs that are suitable for making into cushion covers.

Here, pieces of machine patchwork have been joined with contrasting solid (plain) fabrics. The diagonal seams have then had further appliqués applied to them to add richness and pattern. The pretty stenciled design from the spring project section (above left) has been applied in a fan shape to a strongly contrasting silk background.

Likewise, the plum blossom design (right) sits on a ground of richly textured linens, and you could easily make a set of three cushions using the other winter symbols from the Three Friends Screen, (see pages 98–9).

Many designs can be devised using this system. Simply join two contrasting fabrics along a strong diagonal and then appliqué another shape across the seam. The delicate shape of the Snowflake medallion (see page 124) would be ideal for adding a print fabric to a ground of patchwork, while the Pinebark lozenge (see page 117) will add elegance to a design.

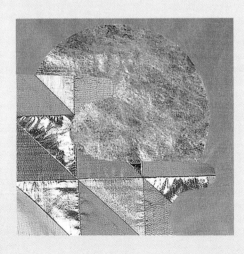

Alternatively, you could use the cloud appliqué pattern (left) to join pieces of patchwork and appliqué. Any combinations of contrasting fabrics can be joined in this way without needing further embellishment.

BOW-TIE BLOCK

The Bow-tie pattern is made from right-angled triangles. Each unit contains four triangles, two of each color. The design is strongest when solid (plain) and print fabrics are alternated in two contrasting colors.

A completed Bow-tie block.

1 Make a Bow-tie triangle template (see page 103), including the marked seam allowance, and use to mark the required number of triangles on your chosen fabrics. For this block you will need eighteen of fabric A, six of fabric B, six of fabric C, and six of fabric D. Mark the notched seam allowances in each corner of every patch with a soft pencil. (Experienced quilters may find notching unnecessary.)

2 Cut out the patches with a pair of scissors. You should have 36 in total.

3 Join the solid (plain) and print patches together in pairs using a 1 cm (⅜ in) seam allowance. Press the seams to one side on the back for light fabrics and press the seams open on the back for heavy fabrics.

4 Pin two pairs together at the center and at both ends, matching seams carefully. Machine stitch together. Press the seams to one side for light fabrics and press the seams open for heavy fabrics. Join the resulting Bow-tie units in rows, then join the rows to complete the block.

The Bow-tie block features in the Noble Medallion Throw (pp.82–5).

PINWHEEL BLOCK

The Pinwheel block works best when two strongly contrasting fabrics are combined to create a mass of turning triangles. Each unit is made up of eight right-angled triangles, four of each color.

A completed Pinwheel block.

1 Trace the Pinwheel triangle template (see page 103), including the marked seam allowance, and use to mark the required number of triangles on your chosen fabrics. For this block you will need sixteen of fabric A, and four each of fabrics B, C, D, and E. Mark the notched seam allowances in each corner with a soft pencil. (Experienced quilters may find notching unnecessary.)

2 Cut out the patches. You should have 32 in total.

3 Join the solid (plain) and print triangles in pairs to form squares, using a 1 cm (⅜ in) seam allowance. Press seams to one side for light fabrics and open for heavy fabrics. Join the squares to form four rows, alternating the colors as shown. Press the block.

4 Join the four rows in the correct order, matching seams carefully.

The Pinwheel block features in the Noble Medallion Throw (pp.82–5).

CHEVRON BLOCK

For this pattern, place the templates face up when cutting the patches for rows 1, 3, 5, and 7 and face down when cutting the patches for rows 2, 4, 6, and 8.

A completed Chevron block.

1 Trace the three shapes from page 104, including the marked seam allowance, and make the templates according to the instructions on page 25. Mark the top side of each template with a cross. For strips 1, 3, 5, and 7, place the templates face up on the fabric and mark and cut out one long strip, five chevrons, and one corner triangle. For strips 2, 4, 6, and 8, place the templates face down on the fabric and mark and cut one long strip, five chevrons, and one corner triangle.

2 Using a 1 cm (⅜ in) seam allowance, make eight pieced strips by joining the patches together in the correct order. Arrange the strips in your chosen pattern, ready for piecing.

3 Join strips 1–4 in sequence. Join strips 5–8 . Turn strips 5–8 180 degrees so that the long strip is at the top. Join this strip to strips 1–4 .

The Chevron block features in the Tree Peony Cushion (pp.64–5)

SUN AND SHADE BLOCK

This is made from two pieced triangles, one in light shades and one in dark shades. Each pieced triangle contains four strips of print fabric, which are cut using the templates on page 106.

A completed Sun and Shade block.

1 Trace the four shapes from page 106, including the marked seam allowance, and make the templates (see page 25). Mark the notched seam allowances in each corner with a soft pencil. (Experienced quilters may find notching unnecessary.)

2 Cut out the required number of fabric patches. For each Sun and Shade block you will need one of each shape in dark contrasting prints and one of each shape in light contrasting prints.

3 Using a 1 cm (⅜ in) seam allowance, join the four dark shapes in the correct order to form a large pieced triangle. Join the light strips in the same way.

4 Pin the two resulting pieced triangles right sides together along their long edges. Machine stitch together, then press the seams to one side for light fabrics and press open for heavy fabrics.

The Sun and Shade block features in the Sun and Shade Kimono (pp.74–5).

Machine Appliqué

THIS TECHNIQUE INVOLVES LAYING ONE FABRIC on top of another and stitching the raw edges in position, either visibly, using a decorative stitch, or invisibly, using monofilament. Although appliqué is not, strictly speaking, a patchwork technique, it has been included in this section because most of the blocks of appliqué patterns featured in the projects resemble patchwork once they have been stitched together. Notice how the Ribbon Hexagon Star (above left) resembles the patchwork Hexagon Star on page 20 and the Wave Block (right) resembles the traditional Clamshell block.

There are various ways of securing multiple layers of fabric together. I like to mount my fabrics on paper-backed fusible web to give them extra stability during assembly. The simplest and most commonly used method of finishing the raw edges is the zigzag stitch, which can give a solid line of stitching when it is set close together. Other more decorative finishes include satin stitch, which gives a slightly embossed look, and hand-embroidered herringbone stitch for a loose, homespun finish. The stitching can either be worked in a contrasting color (see left) or in a matching color for a more subtle finish. You can also choose from a range of metallic threads, which look very effective on lustrous fabrics.

Small Construction shown

1 Construction for the small basket shown: Sew 4-2½" squares together to make one row. Make 4 rows. Combine the rows.

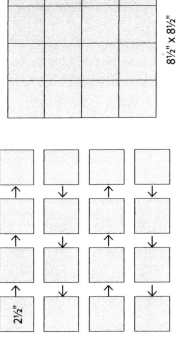

8½" x 8½"

2½"

2 Fuse the fusible to the wrong side of the squares. Layer the squares and Lining right sides together. Sew around the edge. Leave an opening for turning. Turn right sides out.

leave opening

Fusible 8" x 8"

Lining

Fusible 8" x 8"

3 Sew the corner squares on the seam lines. Top stitch the edge and corners down a shown in the photograph.

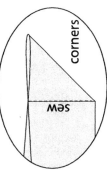

corners

sew

2

ABC 123

Moda fabric:

ABC 123

by: American Jane

Size small:

Moda Candy:
16-2½" x 2½" squares

Lining:
1-8½" x 8½" square

Fusible:
1-8" x 8" square

Size large:

Moda Candy:
36-2½" x 2½" squares

Lining:
1-12½" x 12½" square

Fusible:
1-12" x 12" square

(instructions are not shown for the large size)

······ RIBBON HEXAGON STAR BLOCK ·····

For this technique, the template is cut to the finished size with no seam allowances added. Narrow ribbon is applied to the finished block to define the hexagon star pattern.

*A completed
Ribbon Hexagon Star block.*

1 Trace the hexagon shape from page 104 and make a cardboard template. Cut four long strips of fabric the same width as the hexagon template plus 5 mm (¼ in) seam allowances. For this block you will need one of fabric A, one of fabric B, one of fabric C, and one of fabric D. Join the strips in the correct order and press seams to one side for light fabrics and press open for heavy fabrics.

2 Draw around the hexagon template the required number of times onto the fabric strips to make rows of hexagons interspersed with triangles. Use a ruler to make sure that the diagonal lines on each row align exactly with the rows beneath.

3 Select a ribbon, 5 mm (¼ in) wide, and pin first along the diagonal lines, then the horizontal lines. Trim even with the sides.

4 Baste the ribbon in place without removing the pins.

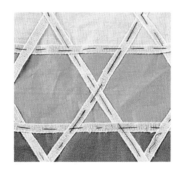

5 Machine stitch over your rows of basting, removing pins as you stitch.

The Ribbon Hexagon Star block features in the Summer Dawn Screen (pp.66–9).

······ EMBROIDERED HEXAGON STAR BLOCK ··

Although similar in appearance to the previous design, it allows for more intricate designs. This technique is more time-consuming since the appliquéd triangles are cut out individually and machine embroidered in place.

*A completed
Embroidered Hexagon Star block.*

1 Trace the hexagon and triangle shapes from page 104 and make the templates from cardboard.

2 Cut three long strips of fabric the same width as the hexagon template plus 5 mm (¼ in) seam allowances. For this block, you will need two of fabric A and one of fabric B. Draw around the hexagon template onto the fabric strips the required number of times to create a repeat pattern.

3 Cut five long strips of fabric C the same width as the triangle template plus seams. Draw around the triangle template the required number of times to create a repeat pattern.

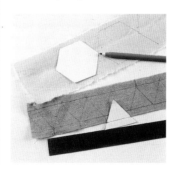

4 Mount the five triangle strips on paper-backed fusible web. Cut out the triangles, adding a 5 mm (¼ in) seam allowance along one edge only. Position the triangles on the hexagon strips and iron in place.

5 Cut away the seam allowance along one long edge of the first strip (A). Position the cut edge on strip B, matching the pattern, and machine embroider using satin stitch in contrasting thread. Cut away the seam allowance on the lower edge of strip B and position on the remaining strip A. Machine embroider in the same way. Embroider the diagonal rows.

The Embroidered Hexagon Star block features in the Water Iris Cushion (pp.48–9) and the Summer Dawn Screen (pp. 66–9).

WAVE BLOCK

For this appliqué technique, two styles of curved patch are arranged in overlapping sequence on a foundation fabric square. A variety of fabrics can be used for the large waves, but it is best to limit the smaller waves to one solid (plain) color only.

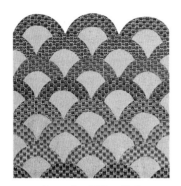

A completed Wave block.

1 Trace the two wave shapes from page 105 and use to cut two templates with 5 mm (¼ in) seam allowances added, from stiff cardboard (see page 25).

2 Back your chosen fabrics with paper-backed fusible web before cutting out the required number of large waves and small waves from solid (plain) and print fabrics. Mark the notched seam allowances in each corner with a soft pencil.(Experienced quilters may find notching unnecessary.)

3 Cut a piece of foundation fabric the required size from muslin (calico). Use a pencil and ruler to mark the center with a vertical line.

4 Remove the backing from the fusible web and position the first large wave over the center mark. Iron in place to fuse the layers together. Position more large waves on either side and iron in place, then arrange the small waves inside to complete the first row. Arrange the remaining large and small waves in rows in the same way.

5 When all the waves are fused in place, machine appliqué the curved edges using a small zigzag stitch in invisible monofilament. Trim the sides of the block if necessary to form a square.

The Wave block features in the Summer Dawn Screen (pp. 66–9).

CRAZY PATCHWORK BLOCK

This style of patchwork is ideal for using up scraps of fabric. I chose an assortment of plaids, stripes, solids (plains), and prints in coordinating colors for this block, which I mounted on paper-backed fusible web to provide extra stability during assembly.

A completed Crazy Patchwork block.

1 Select a variety of coordinating fabrics and cut them into random-shaped pieces using a rotary cutter or scissors. Back each fabric patch with paper-backed fusible web ready for assembly.

2 Cut a foundation square the required size plus 5 mm (¼ in) seam allowances from muslin (calico). Use a water-soluble marker and ruler to draw in the seam allowances on all sides.

3 Starting in the top left-hand corner, begin to arrange your fabric patches on the foundation fabric square, overlapping the patches by 5 mm (¼in).

4 When you are happy with the overall pattern, remove the paper backing from the fabric patches and iron them lightly in position. Don't worry if the patches overlap the seam allowances slightly at the sides; these can be trimmed away later.

5 The patches can be secured to the foundation fabric in various ways. Here they are being machine stitched using a small zigzag stitch in matching thread, but you may prefer to use invisible monofilament or a decorative hand embroidery stitch such as herringbone.

Crazy patchwork features in the Three Friends Screen (pp. 98–9) and the Crazy Patchwork Cushion (pp. 58–9).

CLOUDY FAN BLOCK

A "window" template is ideal for cutting out large shapes such as the fan,
since it enables you to view the ground fabric before you actually cut it out. This technique is especially useful
when cutting patches from fabrics with large motifs, including
upholstery fabrics.

A completed Cloudy Fan block.

3 Select a contrasting fabric for the clouds – here we have used a solid (plain) brocade. Use your cloud templates to cut out one of each motif in the same fabric. Back each shape with paper-backed fusible web.

4 Remove the paper backing from the clouds and position where marked on the fan. Iron in place to fuse the layers together.

5 Carefully cut out the fan along the marked lines using scissors.

6 Machine appliqué the scalloped raw edges of each cloud motif using a narrow zigzag stitch in invisible monofilament, or you could use satin stitch in a matching color if preferred.

7 Cut a contrasting piece of background fabric 30 cm (12 in) square plus 5 mm (¼ in) seam allowances and position the Cloudy Fan on top, aligning the raw edges of two sides only. Baste the Cloudy Fan in position along both curved edges.

8 Machine appliqué the two curved edges of the fan using narrow zigzag stitch in monofilament. The fan can either be left as it is, or finished with herringbone stitch in a contrasting pearl cotton thread (see page 40).

1 Trace and enlarge the solid fan and two cloud motifs from pages 108–9 and cut out the shapes. Cut a piece of cardboard the same size as your finished block plus 5 mm (¼ in) seams [here 30 cm (12 in) square], position the fan in the center, and draw around the shape. Position the two cloud shapes inside the solid fan and draw around them. Cut out the cloud motifs with a craft knife, then cut out the fan shape to give a "window" template.

2 Position the fan template on the right side of the fabric and move it around in order to find the most interesting area of the design. This technique of using a "window" template is especially useful for cutting shapes out of upholstery fabrics with large patterns, since a conventional template would shield the design. Mark the fan shape on the fabric, then position and mark the clouds inside the fan.

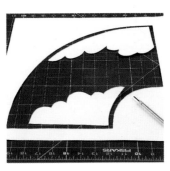

The Cloudy Fan features in the Spring Fans Screen (pp.50–3), the Crazy Fan Bedspread (pp.62–3), and the Cloudy Fan Cushion (pp.76–7).

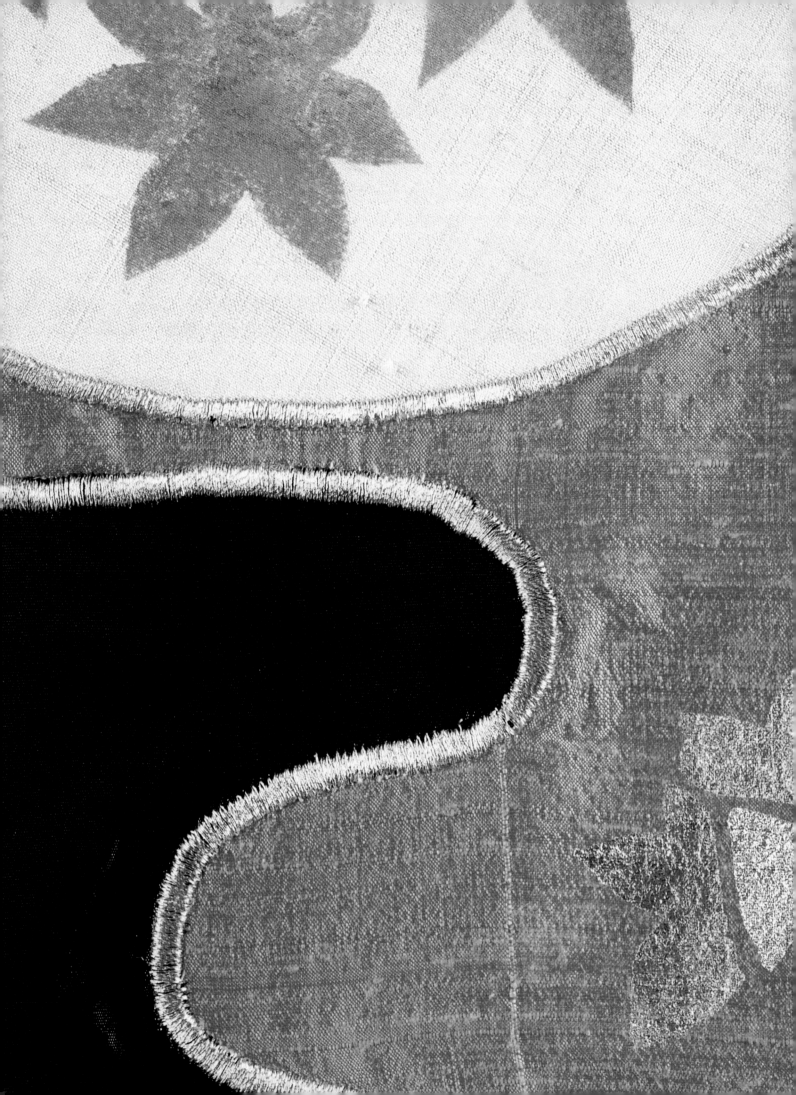

decorative techniques

Decorative Techniques

THE RICHNESS OF JAPANESE TEXTILES derives from the multiplicity of decorative techniques that are used to create them. In essence, these techniques are simple, but when several are combined on one piece, they create ornate and varied designs. In the following pages I have put together a basic set of decorative techniques that can be practiced at home without too much specialist knowledge or equipment. Some of the crafts – such as stenciling – you may have tried before, although not necessarily on fabric. The interesting thing about all these techniques is that you can keep them very simple, by using only one or two stencils combined with simple patchwork or appliqué, or you can create a highly complex result with several finishes at once. Stenciling is a craft that is shared by both East and West. A special feature of Japanese stenciling, or *katazome,* is the subtle blending of one color into another to create

hazy, multicolored designs. One of the ways to create an instant Oriental look is the process known as dip-dyeing, which has been seen in Japanese prints, paintings, and fabrics throughout history. Another ancient technique is gilding, or *surihaku,* which has been used to decorate kimonos throughout the ages. Traditional Oriental embroidery is universally admired. Here we have concentrated on two basic stitches – long and short stitch and couching – which are very effective for depicting natural forms.

DIP-DYEING

In this technique, the fabric is only partly immersed in the dye to achieve a color that fades from light to dark. It is very simple to do and gives an instant Oriental look. Cold-water dyes are suited only to natural fibers such as silk, wool, cotton, or linen, which will absorb the dye evenly. Cold-water, fiber-reactive dyes are available in powder or liquid form in a spectrum of different colors.

Dip-dyed silk. Note how the color fades gradually from light to dark without an obvious tide-line.

1 If the fabric is new, wash it in detergent to remove any manufacturer's finishes and rinse it carefully. Mark the sides of the fabric with thread to show the upper limit of the dye – that is, where you want the color to fade to.

2 Choose a dyebath that is large enough to accommodate the width of the fabric without too much folding, and deep enough to hold the fabric when it is submerged in the dye. Mix a weak solution of cold-water dye using about a third of the usual strength indicated on the packet.

3 Next, wet the fabric in clean water and secure it on a wooden rod. Dip the bottom end of the fabric into the dyebath.

4 Keeping the bottom end of the fabric submerged in the dye, move the fabric constantly up and down in the dyebath until it has absorbed enough dye to cover your selected area. When the correct depth of color is achieved – remember that a wet color can be up to seven times darker than when dry – remove the fabric from the dyebath and rinse it immediately under cold running water. Hang the fabric on a clothesline to dry so that the undyed area is at the top. Fix the dyes by ironing.

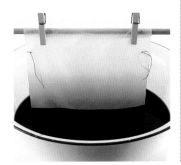

Dip-dyeing features in the Water Iris Cushion (pp.48–9), the Summer Dawn Screen (pp.66–9), and the Mist and Snow Bedcover (pp.94–7).

TRACING AND CUTTING STENCILS

The best material to use for cutting stencils is stencil card or acetate, which can be bought from craft stores. You will also need a sharp craft knife or scalpel and a cutting mat or similar non-slip surface. All of the motif designs in this book have been designed so that they can be adapted for stenciling (page 38), embroidery (page 40), or gilding (page 39).
Templates are on pages 112–6.

A cut-out stencil of a dragonfly. Note the detailed cutting along the body.

1 Photocopy your chosen motif from pages 112–6, reducing or enlarging it if necessary. Carefully trace the motif onto tracing paper, using a soft pencil.

2 Take a piece of stencil card the required size and place a piece of transfer paper on top. Position the tracing right side up on the transfer paper. Trace over the marked lines through both layers of paper onto the stencil card beneath. Remove the papers and, if necessary, retouch the outline of the motif with a pencil.

3 Anchor the stencil card to a cutting mat with masking tape to prevent it from moving around. Using a sharp craft knife or scalpel, cut "windows" out of the card where the stencil paint is to be applied.

4 Continue cutting out the shapes, taking care not to cut through any of the "bridges" that connect the "windows" as these help to strengthen the stencil.

Stenciling features in the Water Iris Cushion (pp. 48–9), the Spring Fans Screen (pp.50–3), the Summer Dawn Screen (pp.66–9), and the Gilded Maple Leaf Screen (pp.78–81).

STENCILING

Choose ready-mixed fabric dyes that are fixed by ironing since these can be used on both natural and man-made fibers. The following eight colors should be sufficient to print the stencils in this book: reds (Fuchsia/Crimson and Scarlet); yellows (Chrome and Ocher); blues (Ultramarine and Deep Turquoise); Black and White. You may also need a strong Moss Green, although this color can be created by mixing Deep Turquoise with Chrome Yellow. You will also need at least three small stencil brushes – one for each major color in the design. Always test the colors on a scrap of fabric beforehand and bear in mind that they will appear much darker and more intense when they are wet. Keep plenty of absorbent paper towels on hand for blotting your brush.

A stenciled dragonfly. Note how the colors are overlaid to create subtle variations in tone.

1 Use masking tape to secure your fabric to a padded surface ready for printing – an ironing board, protected with several layers of fabric, is an ideal surface because the fabric layers will soak up any excess dye. Position your stencil over the fabric and secure it in place with masking tape.

2 Dip a stencil brush into the palest color and dab off any excess dye on a piece of absorbent paper. Stipple lightly and evenly over your selected area, building up the color gradually until the fabric "windows" are the desired depth of color.

3 Take a clean stencil brush and apply the second (deeper) color in the same way as the first. Remember to keep the brush as dry as possible by blotting it on absorbent paper, or the dye will bleed underneath the stencil and create a blurred image. There is no need to leave the colors to dry between applications because they are

fairly dry anyway. Stencil the remaining areas of cloth, using a clean brush for each color. Finish with the darkest color.

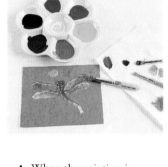

4 When the printing is complete, carefully remove the stencil and leave the fabric to dry. When dry, fix the dyes by ironing the fabric on the reverse, following the manufacturer's instructions.

THE COLOR WHEEL

This photograph shows how your six basic colors can be mixed together to create subtle variations in tone. If you are stenciling over a large area, it is a good idea to try out your chosen colors first and practice blending the colors. Try creating a color wheel such as this on a spare piece of fabric and using it as a reference.

Stenciling features in the Water Iris Cushion (pp.48–9), the Spring Fans Screen (pp.50–3), the Summer Dawn Screen (pp.66–9), the Gilded Maple Leaf Screen (pp.78–81), and the Crazy Patchwork Cushion (pp.58–61).

GILDING

Gold or silver patterning, known as surihaku *in Japan, is a very popular feature of traditional kimonos, where it was often included to mimic the more expensive woven cloths that had real gold and silver threads incorporated into their designs. In the No theater tradition, gold signifies a young woman and silver symbolizes an older woman.*

The traditional method of applying gold and silver leaf is using glue or size to anchor the layers of metal, but I prefer to use a simpler approach which involves using paper-backed fusible web to fix the metal leaf in place. Metal leaf is available in many finishes, including gold, silver, and copper, from craft stores or art suppliers.

A gilded house martin.

4 Gently peel away the paper backing to reveal the layer of metal leaf beneath. You may find it useful to dust your hands with talc to prevent the gold leaf from sticking to your fingers.

5 Use a soft brush to smooth the metal leaf onto the surface, dabbing it gently rather than wiping it to prevent it from tearing. Carefully remove any surplus foil from around the edges of the motif.

1 Trace your chosen motif from pages 118–23 and transfer it onto the paper side of a piece of fusible web. Place the fusible web on a cutting mat and cut out the motif with a sharp craft knife, scalpel, or scissors.

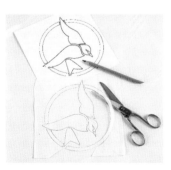

2 Position the motif adhesive-side down on your fabric. Secure the motif in place by pressing the paper side with an iron, following the manufacturer's instructions. Remove the paper backing from the fusible web.

3 Gently lift a sheet of metal foil from its packing and cut a sufficient amount to cover the entire motif. Place the metal foil, paper-side up, over the adhesive motif and press lightly with a warm iron. Remove the backing paper.

Gilding features in the Gilded Maple Leaf Screen (pp.78–81), the Shimmering Wallhanging (pp.90–1), and the Crazy Patchwork Cushion (pp.58–61).

EMBROIDERING MOTIFS

Embroidery is an ideal way of enhancing your designs and giving them a refined and elegant finish. Natural images, such as insects and flowers, are widely used on kimonos and obi, and I have included several templates at the back of the book (see pages 112–6). Long and short stitch (right) is ideal for depicting natural forms. I use stranded silk thread, working with one or two strands of silk in my needle at a time for refined stitching and blending.

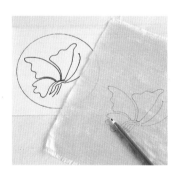

An embroidered butterfly.

1 Trace your chosen motif from the back of the book and transfer it onto fabric using a water-soluble marker or carbon paper.

2 Stretch the fabric over an embroidery hoop and outline the design in backstitch using one strand of thread in a mid-tone color.

3 Beginning with the darkest shade of your first color, work the first row of long and short stitch, radiating the stitches from the center of the design. Continue with the bricking effect so that each line of stitching merges with the one above and below it. You will need at least three or four shades of each color for a successful blend.

4 Work the remaining areas of the design, taking care to cover the outlining back stitches.

Embroidery features in the Tree Peony Cushion (pp.64–5) and the Crazy Patchwork Cushion (pp.58–61).

LONG AND SHORT STITCH

1 For long and short stitch, come up at A, go down at B, up at C, and down at D. Continue alternating between long and short stitches.

2 Continue with the bricking effect so that each row merges with the row directly above or below it.

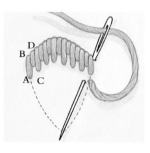

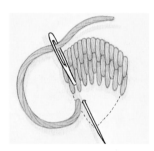

COUCHING STITCH

1 To couch a piece of upholstery cord, bring it through the fabric at A ready for stitching down.

2 Thread your needle with embroidery thread, come out at B, go down at C, and out again at D.

3 Continue couching the cord, forming small stitches at right angles to the laid thread.

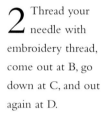

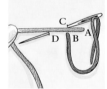

HERRINGBONE STITCH

1 Come up at A, go down at B, come up at C. Cross down and insert at D, coming up at E.

2 Cross up and insert at F, then come up at G. Pull through. Threads will cross at the bottom.

3 Cross down and insert at H, up at I. Continue along the row, repeating steps 1 and 2.

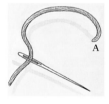

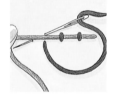

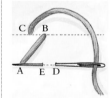

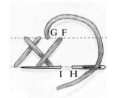

APPLIQUÉ MOTIFS

The modern method of fusible appliqué is developed from the traditional technique of using paste to secure fabric motifs before they are finally edged in place with embroidery stitches. The main advantage of fusing is that it is quick, and today it can be speeded up with the use of paper-backed fusible web. It also eliminates the need to turn under the raw edges of the fabric, allowing you to use more complicated motifs. Once an appliquéd motif has been bonded to the *background fabric, it should be secured around the edges with stitching. The most commonly used finish in this book is machine zigzag stitch using invisible monofilament, which gives a tough, seamless finish that is strong enough to withstand washing on household items such as bedcovers. On smaller-scale motifs, you may prefer to use a machine embroidery stitch such as satin stitch or a hand embroidery stitch in silk or pearl cotton.*

An appliquéd flower.

Above: An alternative method of finishing the raw edges of the appliqué is using a narrow satin stitch in matching embroidery thread. This gives an attractive embossed finish.

4 Peel the paper backing off the motif and position it on your background fabric. Iron in place to fuse the layers together.

5 Machine stitch close to the raw edges of the motif, using a medium zigzag stitch and invisible monofilament.

1 Cut a piece of iron-on fusible web the same size as your chosen appliqué motif. Following the manufacturer's instructions, carefully bond the glue side onto the wrong side of your chosen appliqué fabric. This will give the fabric extra stability during assembly.

2 Trace the motif onto tracing paper. Take a piece of dressmaker's carbon paper and lay it face down on the right side of the appliqué fabric. Place the paper tracing on top. Go over the outline with a sharp pencil on a firm surface. Alternatively, transfer the motif by tracing directly onto the paper side of the fusible web.

3 If necessary, touch up the outline of the motif with a water-soluble pen. Cut out the motif with sharp scissors. The petals on this flower are cut out individually, but most of the motifs can be cut out in one piece. Note: You can reverse the motif design by tracing over the back of the tracing paper rather than the front.

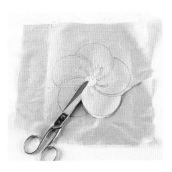

Appliqué features in the Spring Fans Screen (pp.50–3), the Tree Peony Cushion (pp.64–5), the Cloudy Fan Cushion (pp. 76–7), the Gilded Maple Leaf Screen (pp.78–81), the Noble Medallion Throw (pp.82–5), the Mist and Snow Bedcover (pp. 94–7), and the Three Friends Screen (pp.98–9).

PROJECTS

SPRING

SPRING IS the season of cherry blossom viewing, and picnics held under the trees when the petals start to fall and flutter like pink and white confetti. The cherry, or *sakura*, is Japan's national flower because it dies so beautifully at the peak of its perfection.

The fresh spring winds make kite flying exciting, and they are flown for both festivals and sport. There are many different shapes and sizes of kites: tortoise, carp, and crane shapes; kites as big as three men or as small as sparrows; some painted with the faces of famous actors, others with poems and good-luck symbols written on them to send into the sky as messages to the gods.

The natural world is celebrated in all its freshness and delicacy, and the same clear, vibrant colors and designs are used in the following projects. The fabrics are crisp cottons, favorite indigo blue and white, sky blues, and small scale prints, or patterned silks, brilliant as festival kimonos, and stitched together to make inspiring designs.

Flying Kites Quilt

THE JAPANESE WORD FOR KITE *(tako) is a combination of the words for "wind" and "cloth." Flying kites is a national pastime for people of all ages in Japan. Here familiar diamond shaped kites fly across a child's sky-blue bedcover.*

BLOCKS

You will need nine pieced kite blocks and 15 solid (plain) background squares. Each finished block = 30 cm (12 in) square. Finished size of quilt = 120 x 180 cm (48 x 72 in).

RIGHT: **Kite block**

The kite is pieced from alternating Japanese prints, set against a blue background.

FAR RIGHT: **Strings**

Bias-tape kite strings are appliquéd to ten of the solid (plain) background squares.

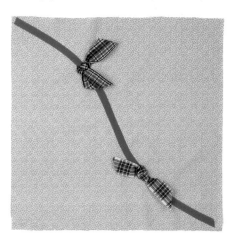

FABRICS

Background fabric: printed cotton in six shades of the same color, progressing from dark (fabric A) to light (fabric F)

Kite blocks: small-scale Japanese prints (for example, polka dots, stripes, and plaids), in bright contrasting colors that will show up against the background fabric

Kite strings: bias tape, 1 cm (¹/₂ in) wide

Ties: plaid ribbons in assorted bright colors, 2.5–5 cm (1–2 in) wide

Please refer to the Order of Work for specific piece sizes

ORDER OF WORK

1 Cut 15 background squares, 30 cm (12 in) across plus 5 mm (¼ in) seam allowances, from background fabric. You will need two of the darkest color (fabric A), three of fabric B, three of fabric C, one of fabric D, three of fabric E, and three of the lightest color (fabric F).

2 Photocopy the templates for the kite block from page 107 and enlarge to the correct size. Cut out and piece together the nine kite blocks, using two contrasting prints for each kite and background fabrics A–F for the sky, including the marked 1 cm (⅜ in) seam allowance,

BELOW: **Ribbons**

The kite strings are tied with plaid ribbons.

3 Using the photograph (see opposite) as a guide, mark the position of the kite strings on ten of the solid (plain) background squares. Use tailor's chalk to draw a wavy, diagonal line that starts in the top left-hand corner and finishes in the bottom right-hand corner. Pin the bias tape along the marked lines and cut to fit. Cut the plaid ribbons into 15 cm (6 in) lengths and pin two pieces under each bias-tape kite string.

4 Appliqué the kite strings in position by zigzag stitching down each side of the bias tape using monofilament thread. Knot the ribbon ties securely over the tape.

5 Assemble the quilt by stitching the blocks together in the correct order (see opposite). Press the seams open. The quilt top is now ready for backing.

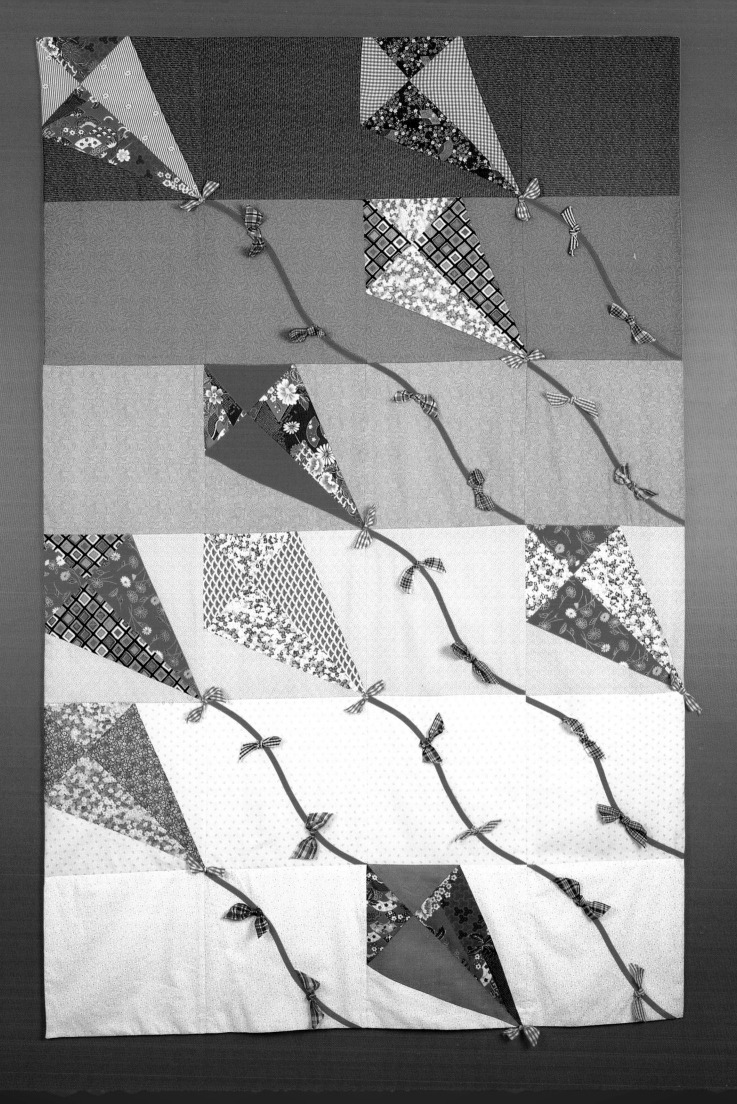

Water Iris Cushion

THE IRIS IS A SYMBOL OF SPRING, *and it can often be found beside streams and rivers.*

Here the riverbank is represented by the curved edge of the hexagon star appliqué, and the

water by shimmering silk in blues and greens.

FABRICS

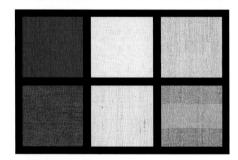

Habotai silk for dip-dyeing and stenciling

Solid (plain) and striped silks in pale blue, cream, green, mauve, and purple

Please refer to the Order of Work for specific piece sizes

TOP RIGHT: **Dip-dyed stenciled square**
Plain habotai silk is dip-dyed in indigo dye before stenciling with iris and dragonfly.

RIGHT: **Hexagon star appliqué**
This is made using the machine-appliqué method on page 31. It is then trimmed to size.

BLOCKS AND STENCILS

You will need one piece of hexagon star appliqué, one dip-dyed stenciled square, one iris template, and one dragonfly template.
Finished size of cushion = 45 cm (18 in) square.

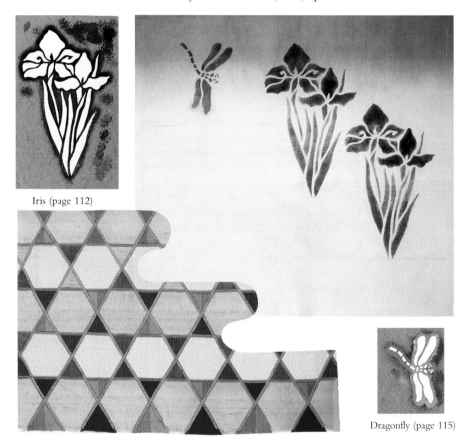

Iris (page 112)

Dragonfly (page 115)

ORDER OF WORK

1 Take a sheet of paper the same size as your finished cushion plus seams, and draw on it the curved edge of the riverbank.

2 Trace the hexagon and triangle templates from page 104. Cut five strips of silk 45 x 6 cm (17½ x 2½ in), three in pale blue and two in cream. Mark the hexagons' position on the silk strips (see page 31).

3 Cut out the required number of triangles from contrasting silks and back with paper-backed fusible web. Iron in place on the silk strips. Machine appliqué the strips together in alternating sequence, using satin stitch and contrasting thread (see page 31). Use the paper pattern to trace the curve of the riverbank onto the assembled block and cut along the marked line.

4 Cut the habotai silk to the same size as your finished cushion. Dip-dye the top quarter in blue (see page 37). Trace the curved riverbank onto the dyed silk with a water-soluble pen and stencil the irises and dragonfly (see page 38).

5 Position the hexagon star appliqué on the dyed silk and machine embroider along the curved edge using satin stitch.

Spring Fans Screen

THE VIVID COLORS *of this screen are inspired by the brilliant kimono traditionally worn by young women in Japan. The cherry blossom is the national flower of Japan, and along with the wisteria and iris, it is a symbol of spring.*

BLOCKS

FAR LEFT: Appliqué fan block
Spring flowers and flying insects are stenciled onto cream raw silk in colors to complement the red, purple, and green of the screen. The completed fan is then machine appliquéd onto a brilliant scarlet background

LEFT: Checkerboard block
Silks in the acid green of spring leaves and the deep purple of early spring flowers are chosen for the checkerboard blocks.

FABRICS

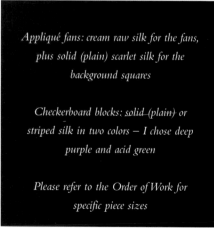

Appliqué fans: cream raw silk for the fans, plus solid (plain) scarlet silk for the background squares

Checkerboard blocks: solid (plain) or striped silk in two colors – I chose deep purple and acid green

Please refer to the Order of Work for specific piece sizes

STENCILS

Peony (page 113)

Butterfly (page 114)

Iris (page 112)

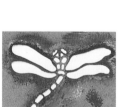

Dragonfly (page 115)

Moth (page 114)

Wisteria (page 112)

BLOCKS

ORDER OF WORK

LEFT: **Blocks**

You will need seven checkerboard blocks and eight appliqué fan blocks. The size of the blocks will be determined by the size of your screen. To estimate the size of each block, measure the total height of your screen. Divide the total height measurement by five and add generous seams. The finished size of my blocks is 30 cm (12 in) square. If preferred, this design could be adapted for a bedcover or wallhanging.

1 Cut eight blocks 30 cm (12 in) square, plus 5 mm (¼ in) seams, from red silk. Cut eight squares of fusible interfacing the same size. Back each silk square with a square of interfacing following the manufacturer's instructions.

2 Photocopy the larger fan template from page 125, enlarging the shape to fit the size of your squares. Use the template to draw eight fan shapes onto the cream raw silk.

3 Photocopy the six stencil templates from pages 112–5, trace the shapes onto stencil card and cut out the motifs with a sharp craft knife. Use the stencils to print the flowers and insects onto the cream fans in your chosen colors (see page 38). We used scarlet for the cherry blossom, and brown, created by mixing ocher with green and red, for the branches. The iris and wisteria flowers are stenciled in a range of deep purples created by mixing purples, blues, and reds together, while the leaves are in shades of ocher and green. The insects are printed in a range of the same colors to give a subtle two-tone effect.

4 When the stencil colors are dry, cut out eight pieces of paper-backed fusible web to the same size as the fan shapes. Bond to the reverse side of each stenciled fan and cut out the fans. Carefully position the fans on the red background squares and press lightly in place.

5 Mark the position of the fan spokes on the background squares, using a water-soluble marker pen. Following the machine embroidery method on page 31, stitch the spokes in contrasting thread using a wide satin stitch. Machine embroider the sides of the fan using a slightly wider zigzag stitch.

6 Make seven checkerboard blocks from purple and green silk, following the instructions for Machine Piecing on page 25. You will need to cut eight 7.5 cm (3 in) squares plus 5 mm (¼ in) seams in each color for each checkerboard block.

7 Assemble the three panels of the screen by machine stitching the checkerboard and fan blocks together in the correct order. Press open the seams on the back. The panels are now ready for backing and mounting.

ABOVE: *Stencil the flowers using a range of purples and blues, stippling lightly into the stalk area so that the greens are subtly blended into the base of the iris flower.*

ABOVE: *The wisteria leaves are made up of yellow, ocher, and lime-green stippled together. Add a small amount to the lowest buds of the flowers before lightly blending in the purple.*

ABOVE: *Rich scarlet and deep pink colors have been used for the petals of the cherry flowers to complement the brilliant red background. The buds are a combination of the leaf-green and pink.*

Katsuri Star Throw

KATSURI IS THE JAPANESE NAME *for a tie-dye technique in which the yarn used for the warp threads of a woven fabric is tied at certain points to resist the dye. The patterns made by this technique can be complex or simple, but all are characterized by their hazy appearance.*

STAR BLOCKS

You will need five compass stars, five hexagon stars, five triangle stars, and ten tortoiseshell stars

FABRICS

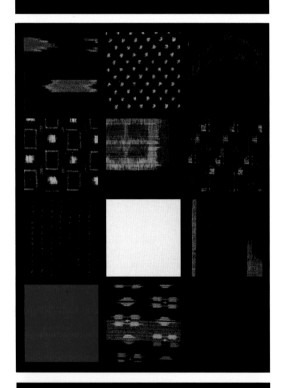

Traditional indigo-dyed or tie-dyed cottons in assorted patterns. Try to keep to deep blue colorings to contrast with the other fabrics

Solid (plain) cotton in red and dark blue

Cream cotton

Please refer to the Order of Work for specific piece sizes

Compass star (page 21)

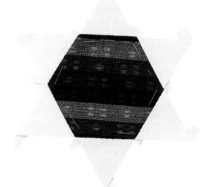

Hexagon star (page 20)

Triangle star (page 20)

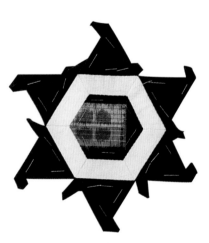

Tortoiseshell star (page 21)

ABOVE: **Star blocks**
The four styles of star block are assembled by hand using backing papers, following the instructions for Hand Piecing on pages 18–21.

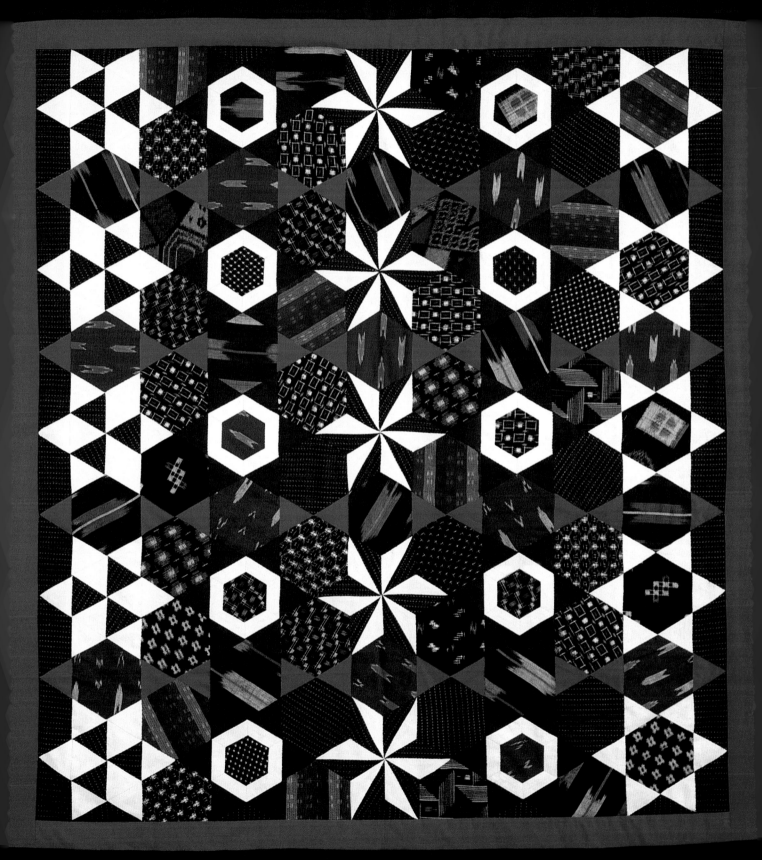

BLOCKS AND BORDER STRIPS

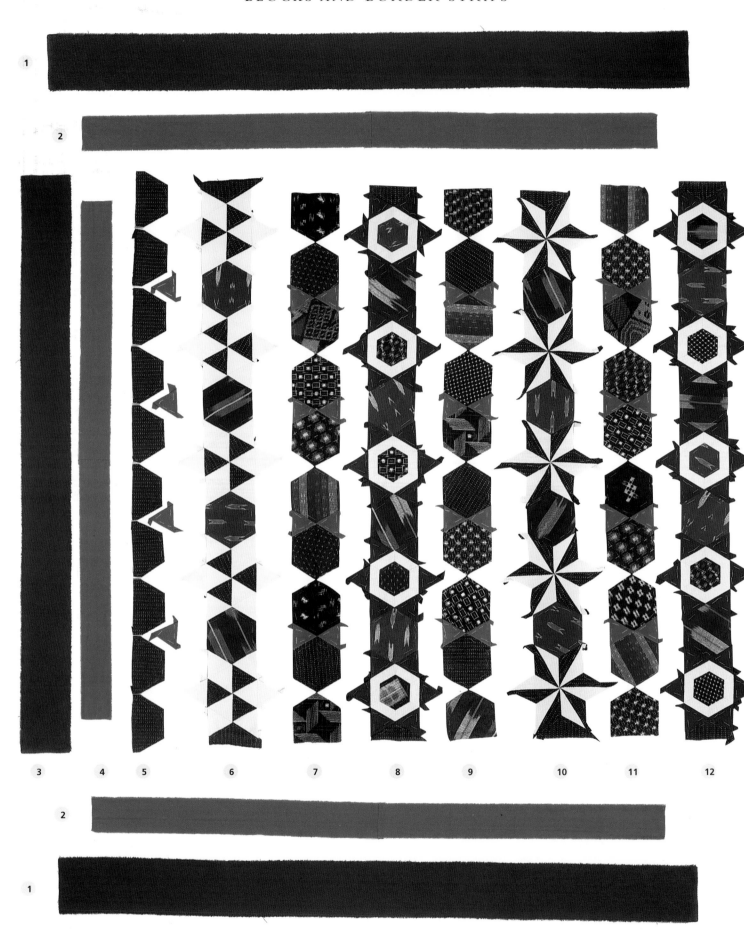

METHODS AND ORDER OF WORK

LEFT: Blocks and Border Strips

The star blocks are made first and then joined into strips, with hexagons and triangles placed in between as fillers. Two wide borders in red and blue complete the quilt. The finished size of the quilt is 167 x 152 cm (66 x 60 in).

13   14   2   1

1 Photocopy the triangle template for the triangle star block from page 102 and cut out the required number of patches, adding 5 mm (¼ in) seam allowances. You will need nine triangles in cream muslin (calico) and three in indigo-dyed cottons. Make five stars, following the instructions for Hand Piecing on page 18. Cut out the remaining shapes for strips 5 and 6, and back with backing papers (see Cutting and Preparing Fabric Patches on page 19). You will need four triangles in red cotton, four hexagons in assorted indigo-dyed cottons, and 12 half-hexagons in dark indigo-dyed cotton. Whipstitch the shapes together in the correct order to make a long strip, placing a half-hexagon at each end and the rest down one side.

2 Photocopy the templates for the tortoiseshell star block from page 102 and cut out the required number of patches, adding 5 mm (¼ in) seam allowances. You will need one small hexagon in indigo-dyed cotton, six quadrilaterals in cream muslin (calico), and six triangles in indigo-dyed cotton. Make ten tortoiseshell stars. Cut out the remaining shapes for strips 8 and 12, and back with backing papers. You will need ten large hexagons in indigo-dyed cotton. Cut two of the large hexagons in half to create four end pieces. Whipstitch the tortoiseshell stars and hexagons together in the correct order to produce two identical strips (No. 8 and 12), placing a half hexagon at each end.

3 Photocopy the template for the compass star block from page 102 and cut out the required number of patches, adding 5 mm (¼ in) seam allowances. You will need six isosceles triangles in cream and six in indigo-dyed cotton. Make five compass stars. Cut out the remaining shapes for strip 10 and back with backing papers. You will need five hexagons in indigo-dyed cotton. Cut one of the indigo-dyed hexagons in half to create two end pieces. Whipstitch the compass stars and hexagons together in the correct order to produce a long strip (No. 10), placing a half hexagon at each end.

4 Photocopy the templates for the hexagon star block from page 102 and cut out the required number of patches, adding seam allowances. You will need six triangles in cream and one hexagon in indigo-dyed cotton. Make five hexagon stars. Cut out the remaining shapes for strip 14 and back with backing papers. You will need four triangles in red cotton, ten hexagons in indigo-dyed cottons, and 12 half-hexagons in indigo-dyed cotton. Whipstitch the hexagon stars, hexagons, half-hexagons, and triangles together in the correct order to produce a long strip (No. 14), placing a half-hexagon at each end and the rest down one side.

5 Photocopy the hexagon and triangle templates for strips 7, 9, 11, and 13 from page 102. Cut out the required number of patches and back with backing papers. You will need eight triangles in red cotton and ten hexagons in contrasting indigo-dyed cottons.

6 On a flat surface, arrange the five star strips in the correct order ready for assembly. Following the photo opposite, whipstitch the hexagons and triangles cut in step 5 to their corresponding star strips. Lightly press with a warm iron before removing the backing papers.

7 Measure the short sides of the quilt top and cut two strips this length, 2 cm (5 in) wide plus 5 mm (¼ in) seam allowances, from red border fabric. Stitch one to each end of the quilt top and open out. Press seams to one side. Measure the long sides of the patchwork and cut two strips this length from red border fabric. Stitch to the sides of the patchwork and open out in the same way.

8 Measure the short sides of the quilt top and cut two pieces of dark blue border fabric this length, making them 10 cm (4 in) wide plus 5 mm (¼ in) seam allowance. Stitch to the short sides of the patchwork, open out, and press seams to one side. Measure the long sides of the patchwork and cut two more pieces of dark blue border fabric this length, making them 10 cm (4 in) wide plus 5 mm (¼ in) seam allowance. Stitch to the long sides of the patchwork and open out. The quilt is now ready for backing.

Crazy Patchwork Cushion

THIS CRAZY PATCHWORK CUSHION *provides a good opportunity for experimenting with different decorative surface treatments, including stenciling, appliqué, hand embroidery, and gilding.*

FABRICS

A selection of metallic silk brocades and solid (plain) silk dupions in pastel colors

Solid (plain) habotai silk for dip-dyeing

Muslin (calico) for backing the patchwork

Please refer to the Order of Work for specific piece sizes

RIGHT: **Decorative motifs**

Motifs are applied in a variety of ways to give the cushion a random "crazy" feel. When selecting stencil paints and/or embroidery threads, try to limit your choice of to three or four coordinating colors to prevent the design from appearing muddled.

DECORATIVE MOTIFS

You will need one stenciled dragonfly, two appliquéd plum flowers, one gilded house martin, one gilded moth and one embroidered butterfly. Finished size of cushion = 45 cm (18 in) square.

Stenciled dragonfly (page 115)

Appliquéd plum blossom (page 123)

Gilded house martin (page 115)

Embroidered butterfly (page 114)

ORDER OF WORK

1 Photocopy the five decorative motifs from the pages shown above right. You will need one butterfly, one moth, one dragonfly, two plum blossoms, and one house martin.

2 Cut eight pieces of silk, each approximately 20 cm (8 in) square. Decorate six of the pieces of silk with your chosen motifs, following the instructions for gilding on page 39, stenciling on page 38, embroidery on page 40, and appliqué on page 41. Dip-dye the remaining two pieces of silk in your chosen colors (see page 37).

3 Cut a foundation square from muslin (calico), 30 cm (12 in) square, plus 5 mm (¼ in) seam allowances. Cut the solid (plain) and decorated silks into random shapes and arrange on the foundation square (see page 32). Machine stitch in monofilament.

4 To finish, decorate the raw edges of each patch by hand with herringbone stitch in metallic thread (see page 40).

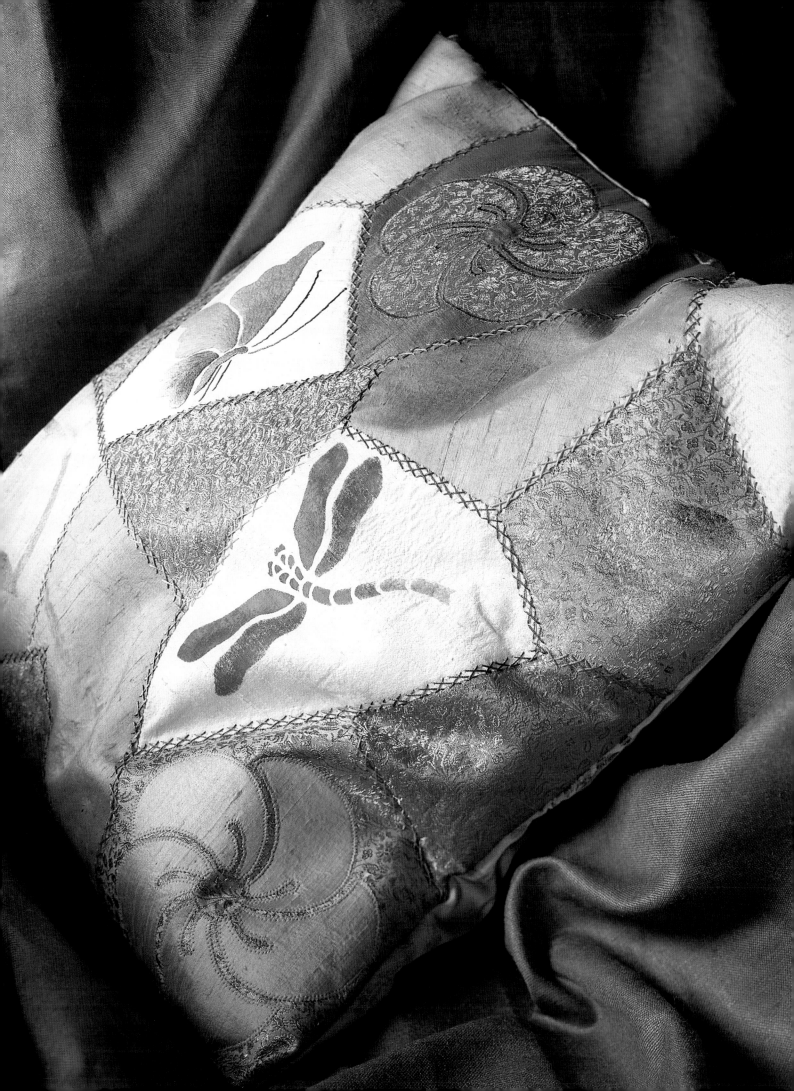

summer

THE HOT, HUMID days of summer need to be taken at a more leisurely pace, to be enjoyed. Traditionally in Japan, fans were used to cool the face, and simple kimonos of white cotton, patterned with indigo dye, were worn by both men and women. Indeed, they are still worn today when people wish to relax.

The folding paper fan is a Japanese invention, born out of the necessity to carry the fan neatly when not in use. It features the art of paper-folding, *origami*, and paper-making, *washi*. Fans depict everything imaginable: paintings of landscapes (often seen through billowing clouds), poems and good luck messages, elegant printed geometric patterns, and, of course, beautiful flying insects and flowers of all the seasons.

The peony, glorious blowsy flower of early summer, is pictured time and again, woven, embroidered, painted, and printed onto furniture, fans, fabrics, and screens to celebrate the richness and abundance of nature.

Crazy Fan Bedspread

IN THIS BEDSPREAD, *Japanese-style appliquéd cloud fans are alternated with traditional striped "crazy" patchwork fans in coordinating colors. The fan outlines and seams of the finished blocks are embroidered with a herringbone stitch in the traditional "crazy" quilt style.*

BLOCKS

You will need 15 striped patchwork fans, 15 appliquéd cloud fans, and 30 solid (plain) background squares. Each block = 30 cm (12 in) square. Finished size of bedspread = 150 cx 180 cm (60 x 72 in).

RIGHT:

Striped fan

The striped fan is pieced from eight toning fan blades in assorted small prints.

FAR RIGHT:

Cloud fan

The solid fan is cut from upholstery fabric, with two cloud motifs appliquéd over the top.

FABRICS

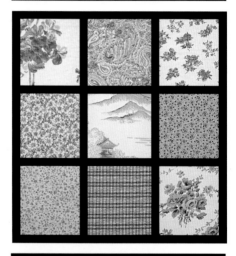

Background fabric: solid-colored (plain) cotton

Solid fans: assorted large prints, from upholstery fabrics

Appliquéd clouds and striped fans: assorted small allover prints to coordinate with the upholstery fabrics

Please refer to the Order of Work for specific piece sizes

ORDER OF WORK

1 Photocopy and enlarge the fan blade template from page 109. Cut the required number of fan blades from assorted small prints. For each striped fan, you will need eight fan blades. Piece them together by machine to make 15 striped fans.

2 Use the fan template as a window template on page 108 to cut 15 solid fans the same size as the striped fans from large-scale upholstery prints.

3 Photocopy and enlarge the two cloud templates from page 108 and cut out 15 of each design from small prints. Bond the back of each shape with iron-on transfer paper. Position the clouds on the solid fans and fuse the two layers together. Zigzag around the raw edges using monofilament.

4 Cut thirty 30 cm (12 in) squares from background fabric, adding 5mm (¼ in) seam allowances.

5 Pin and baste the completed fans to the solid (plain) background squares. Machine appliqué the raw edges of the fans using a zigzag stitch and monofilament.

6 Embroider the inner and outer curves by hand, using herringbone stitch and a contrasting pearl cotton (see page 40).

7 Assemble the quilt top by machine, alternating the cloud and striped fan blocks. Press the seams open on the back.

8 Herringbone-stitch over the seams by hand to finish.

Tree Peony Cushion

THE TREE PEONY *is regarded by both Chinese and Japanese as a noble flower, and it symbolizes riches. Here it is hand embroidered in silk threads on a satin ground, although you may prefer to stencil or appliqué the design using the same template.*

PATCHWORK AND EMBROIDERY

You will need eight patchwork strips for the cushion front, plus a cut-out embroidery.

Finished size of cushion = 41 cm (16 in) square.

RIGHT: **Embroidery**

The tree peony is hand embroidered on a satin ground using long and short stitch, then appliqué to the cushion front and finished with couching.

BELOW CENTER: **Patchwork strips**

Patchwork strips are machine pieced from silk dupions in pastel shades.

FABRICS

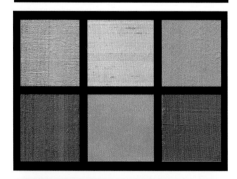

Silk satin for the embroidery ground

Silk threads in assorted colors (we chose four shades of pink and three of green)

Silk dupion in eight pastel colors to complement the embroidery threads

56 cm (22 in) upholstery cord to fit around the outside of the embroidery

Please refer to the Order of Work for specific piece sizes

1

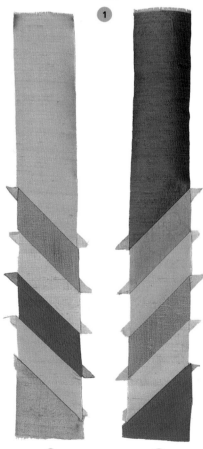

A   B

ORDER OF WORK

1 Transfer the peony template on page 113 onto satin fabric using carbon paper (see page 41). Stretch the satin over a hoop and hand embroider the flower and leaves using long and short stitches (see page 40).

2 Photocopy the chevron patchwork templates from page 104 and enlarge to the correct size. Mark the right side of each template with a cross. Place template A right side up on the silk dupion and use to cut four long strips, one from each of four colors. Turn the template over to give a mirror image and cut four more shapes – one from each of the remaining colors. Use template B to cut 16 chevrons from assorted dupions. Turn the template over to create a mirror image and cut 16 more chevrons from dupions. Use template C to cut four corner triangles, one each from four colors; turn over and cut four more from different colors. Separate the patches into two piles – one containing the mirror images.

3 Machine stitch the patches together in the correct order to form eight pieced strips – four of strip A and four of strip B. Join the strips as shown opposite to create a chevron pattern.

4 Iron a piece of fusible transfer paper to the back of the embroidery. Cut out the peony flower and bud, leaving a 5 mm (¼ in) margin all around. Press down carefully on the patchwork. Machine embroider the raw edges using zigzag stitch in monofilament. Couch with cord to finish.

Summer Dawn Screen

THIS SUMMER SCREEN *is reminiscent of an early morning landscape in rural Japan, with the horizon suffused with rosy pink that pales to white and then deepens to blue. Martins, butterflies, moths, and dragonflies are all regular summer visitors.*

FABRICS

Background fabric for the sky: solid (plain) white cotton or linen for dip-dyeing (we chose a heavy linen for its interesting texture)

Patchwork blocks: small-scale printed cottons in shades of gray and blue for the water; small-scale printed and solid (plain) cottons in shades of olive green for the grass. Choose muted shades to contrast with the brilliance of the sky and organize the colors from dark to light

Muslin (calico) for backing the appliquéd wave blocks

Narrow ribbon for the appliquéd grass

Please refer to the Order of Work for specific piece sizes

STENCILS

BELOW: **Stencils**

The birds and insects are printed in soft grays, greens, and blues to complement the shades of the patchwork. Before cutting out the shapes, you may need to reduce or enlarge them on a photocopier to fit the size of your panels. Stenciling instructions are given on page 38.

Soaring house martin (page 115)

Moth (page 114)

Dragonfly (page 115)

Diving house martin (page 115)

Butterfly (page 114)

Moth (page 114)

BLOCKS

ORDER OF WORK

LEFT: **Blocks**

The size of the blocks will be determined by the size of your screen. My grass and water blocks measure 30 cm (12 in) square plus seams. To estimate the size of the sky panels, measure the total height of the screen. Deduct the combined finished heights of a grass and water block from this measurement, here 60 cm (24 in), and add generous seams. My finished sky panels measure 30 x 90 cm (12 x 36 in).

1 Cut three panels for the sky (blocks 1, 2, and 3) from white background fabric. Dip-dye the top quarter of each panel using mid-blue dye (see page 37). Let them dry before dip-dyeing the lower quarter of each panel with pink dye in the same way.

2 Photocopy the stencil templates from pages 114–5. Trace the shapes onto stencil card and cut out the motifs (see page 37).

3 Using the photograph as a positioning guide, stencil the motifs onto the dyed fabric panels (instructions are on page 38).

4 Cut three pieces of muslin (calico) the same size as the water blocks (4, 5, and 6). Photocopy the two wave templates from page 105 and cut out the required number of patches from gray and blue prints. Back each wave patch with paper-backed fusible web. Starting with the lightest prints at the top, arrange the patches on the cotton squares, overlapping them slightly (see

page 32). Press lightly, then zigzag the raw edges of each patch in monofilament. Trim the sides of each block to form a square.

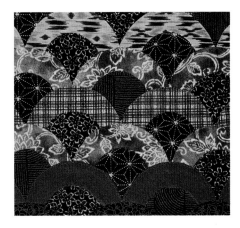

5 Photocopy the hexagon and triangle templates for the grass blocks from page 104. For each grass block, cut five contrasting strips of green printed fabric 33 x 6 cm (13 x 2½ in). Mark the position of the hexagons on the fabric strips (see page 31). Cut out the required number of triangles from solid (plain) fabric and back with paper-backed fusible web. Iron the triangles in position on the fabric strips. Join the strips using the Ribbon Hexagon Star Block method on page 41, substituting machine-stitched ribbon for the zigzag stitching.

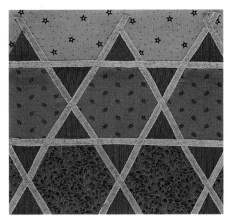

6 Sew a wave block to a grass block, using a flat open seam. Position the wave blocks on the sky panels and machine appliqué using zigzag stitch in monofilament. The panels are now ready for mounting.

ABOVE: *The butterfly is printed in soft shades of blue and green to contrast with the hazy pink background.*

ABOVE: *The house martin is stenciled in dark blues, grays, and browns to stand out against the pink sky. In the photo on the opposite page, see how the stenciled birds have been rotated at different angles to give the scene movement.*

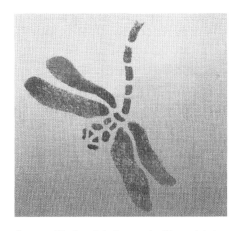

ABOVE: *The dragonfly's wings are printed in muted shades of purple and blue; the body and tail are a rich ocher. Note how the colors are built up in layers to achieve a subtle, two-tone effect.*

Indigo Kimono Quilt

THE REPEATING KIMONO DESIGN *shown here was traditionally used as a method of recycling old, worn kimonos to make new ones. As a patchwork device, it offers endless opportunities for experimenting with different solid (plain) and print fabrics.*

BLOCKS AND SASHING

You will need 12 of each patchwork block, 34 sashing strips, and 35 corner squares.
Finished size of each block = 30 x 34 cm (12 x 13½ in).

(A)

(B)

ABOVE: **Blocks**
There are two styles of patchwork block – one containing print and solid (plain) fabrics(A) and one consisting entirely of mixed prints (B). The two styles are arranged in alternating sequence.

ABOVE: **Sashing**
The vertical sashing strips are interspersed with corner squares, which line up with the horizontal rows of sashing. They also contains the collars of the kimonos.

FABRICS

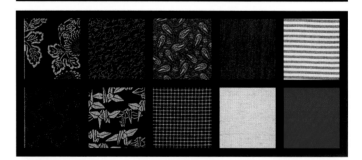

Indigo and deep-blue printed cottons (we used a combination of hand-printed Japanese fabrics and commercial prints)

Solid (plain), indigo-blue cotton

Unbleached muslin (calico)

Sashing: woven stripe in blue and cream

Corner squares: solid (plain) red cotton

Please refer to the Order of Work for specific piece sizes

ORDER OF WORK

1 Photocopy and enlarge the kimono templates from page 111 and cut the required number of patches A, B, C, and D from print fabrics, solid (plain) fabrics, and sashing fabric, including the seam allowance marked on the templates. Make 12 kimonos from print and solid (plain) fabrics (block A) and 12 kimonos from mixed prints (block B).

2 Photocopy and enlarge the sashing strip and corner square templates from page 111. Cut 34 sashing strips from striped fabric, and 35 corner squares from red fabric, including the seam allowance marked on the template.

3 Join six kimono blocks in a vertical row, alternating between blocks A and B by aligning the center back seam of one with the collar point of the next. Join the remaining blocks in the same way to produce four vertical rows in total. Stitch a sashing strip to the lower edge of each row.

4 Join the remaining sashing strips and red corner squares in alternating sequence to form five long strips, each one consisting of six striped strips and seven corner squares.

5 Machine stitch the assembled sashing strips to the rows of kimonos, matching seams carefully so that the horizontal rows of sashing fabric align precisely with the red corner squares. Press the seams to one side on the reverse. The finished quilt is now ready for backing.

FaLL

THE BITTERSWEET atmosphere of fall, the glowing golden light on the glorious colors of dying maple leaves, is seen as a romantic reminder of the passage of time.

Just as we celebrate the harvest moon in songs and poems in the West, so the Japanese celebrate the same seasonal occurrence, with nighttime vigils to watch the moon travel across the sky.

Symbolism plays a large part in all of the decorative Japanese arts, and certain objects signify ideas and messages to the Eastern eye. Although today the use of symbols is not so strictly followed, there are still many motifs that carry their old associations. The curvaceous *choban* symbol, or temple gong, seen on the "noble medallion throw" is the shape of the gong struck in Buddhist temples to tell the time, so its inclusion on a fall fabric refers to the passage of the year, and the *yuki-wa*, or snowflake symbol, is a foretaste of the winter to come.

Sun and Shade Kimono

THIS TROMPE-L'OEIL HANGING looks like a kimono seen from the back. It is a similar size to the real thing and even includes a small padded "collar" made from patchwork triangles. The light and dark fall colors are chosen from solid (plain) and print silks.

BLOCKS

You will need 16 striped blocks and one pieced collar triangle.
Finished size of each striped block = 30 cm (12 in).

LEFT: **Striped block**
Two pieced triangles, one in dark and one in light tones, are joined to make a block.

BELOW: **Collar triangle**
The pointed collar is made from two right-angled triangles.

FABRICS

Assorted necktie fabrics with small allover patterns in dark and light tones

Silk dupions, raw silks, and shot silks in both light and dark tones, to include reds, oranges, ochers, yellows, deep emeralds, and purples, to complement the necktie fabrics

A little batting for the padded collar triangle

Please refer to the Order of Work for specific piece sizes

ORDER OF WORK

1 If you are making the hanging from fabric scraps, photocopy and enlarge the templates on page 106. Cut solid (plain) and print strips in each color, including the seam allowance marked on the templates. Using a 1 cm (⅜ in) seam allowance, join the strips by machine, alternating between solid (plain) and print fabrics. Make 16 striped triangles in light tones and 16 in dark tones. If you are using new fabrics, follow the strip-piecing method of assembly. Start by cutting the fabrics into long strips 5 cm (2 in) wide, plus 1 cm (⅜ in) seams. Join four random dark strips together along their length and four random light strips together, alternating between solid (plain) and print fabrics. Cut into right-angled triangles using a rotary cutter. You will need 16 striped triangles in light tones and 16 in dark tones.

2 Join a light striped triangle to a dark striped triangle, stitching along the long diagonal edge. You should end up with sixteen 30 cm (12 in) squares plus 1 cm (⅜ in) seams.

3 Arrange the blocks in a kimono shape, taking care that the light and dark triangles follow a pattern. Stitch together.

4 Cut two small triangles for the collar, using the template on page 106, and stitch together. Cut a piece of batting and backing the same size and sandwich the three layers together, right sides facing. Stitch around the outside, leaving the lower edge open for turning. Turn right side out. Stitch in place on the kimono matching seams.

Cloudy Fan Cushion

THE FOLDING FAN (sensu) *is often depicted on kimonos and the cloud pattern is often seen on Japanese fans, usually acting as a foil for exotic flowers and decorative motifs. Here a cloud fan of rich Chinese brocades is appliquéd to a patchwork cushion in warm, fall shades.*

BLOCKS

You will need two triangle blocks, one pieced from triangle patches and one pieced from square patches, plus an appliquéd cloud fan. Finished size of cushion = 42 cm (16 in) square.

RIGHT: **Cloud fan**

The solid fan is cut from Chinese brocades of contrasting colors. The palest color is used for the appliquéd clouds.

FAR RIGHT: **Blocks**

The cushion front is made of two hand-pieced triangles – one assembled from triangle patches and one assembled from square patches – which are joined to make a square.

FABRICS

Cloud fan: two contrasting Chinese brocades

Triangle patches: assorted printed necktie fabrics and solid (plain) brocades

Square patches: assorted solid (plain) colored silks, plus a solid (plain) brocade with a repeating flower motif

Please refer to the Order of Work for specific piece sizes

ORDER OF WORK

1 Trace the triangle template from page 109 and cut 16 patches from neck-tie fabrics and 20 from solid (plain) brocades, adding 5 mm (¼ in) seam allowances. Make the triangle block, following the Hand Piecing instructions on page 18. Remove all but the last diagonal row of backing papers. Trim to form a right-angled triangle.

2 Trace the square template from page 109 and cut 16 squares from floral brocade and 20 from plain silks, adding 5 mm (¼ in) seam allowance,. Join by hand (see page 23), alternating the fabrics as shown. Trim to form a triangle.

3 Join the two pieced triangles by hand along their long, diagonal edges. Remove the backing papers.

4 Trace and enlarge the fan template from page 108 and cut out one fan from Chinese brocade. Trace the clouds from page 108–9 and cut the motifs from the palest brocade. Make the fan (see page 33).

5 Machine appliqué the fan onto the cushion front, using satin stitch in contrasting thread.

Gilded Maple Leaf Screen

THE FULL MOON IN FALL *is thought by the Japanese to be particularly beautiful. It was an ancient custom to hold moon-viewing parties where poems were written and read aloud. Here the full moon is shown alongside maple branches and flying cranes, symbols of the fall and longevity.*

FABRICS

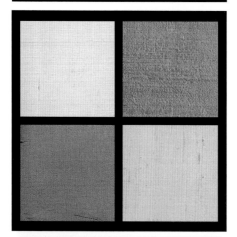

Screen panels: three toning silks, one light, one medium, and one dark, in autumnal shades

Stencil backgrounds: cream raw silk

Moon and falling leaves: gold and silver metal leaf

Please refer to the Order of Work for specific piece sizes

STENCILS

BELOW: **Stencils**
The cranes are stenciled in soft turquoise blue on a cream background, while the maple branches are printed in rich golds and oranges. Individual leaves in gold and silver are gilded directly onto the screen to suggest fluttering leaves in the fall.

Maple branch (see page 116)

Crane (see page 114)

Individual maple leaves (see page 116)

ORDER OF WORK

1 To establish the shape of each block, measure the height and width of one of your screen's panels and cut out a paper pattern the same size, adding extra for seams and for attaching the panels to the screen. Use a ruler to divide the paper pattern into four equal segments. Photocopy the cloud/wave pattern from page 117, enlarging it so that it is the same width as your paper pattern for the screen. Place the cloud template on the paper pattern so that the lowest point of the template aligns with your topmost segment line. Then trace the shape onto the paper pattern. Move the cloud template down to the next line and trace the shape in the same way. Repeat on the third line. Finally, cut along the marked lines to make four paper templates.

BLOCKS

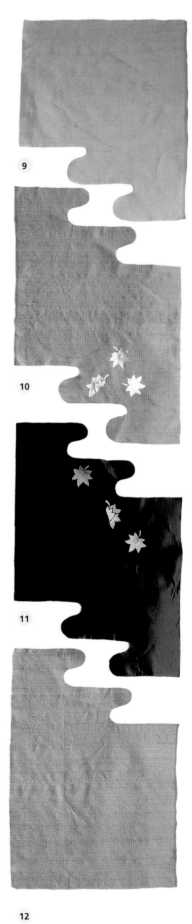

ORDER OF WORK

2 Use your paper templates to cut 12 blocks from background fabrics, making them 5 mm (¼ in) longer top and bottom to allow for seams. We cut five blocks from orange silk, three from gold, and three from black. Note: when you cut the blocks for the center panel, you need to flip the templates over to create a mirror image of each shape.

3 Starting with the left-hand panel, pin, then baste blocks 1 and 2 together along the wavy line, overlapping them by 6 mm (¼ in). Cut a circle 18 cm (7 in) in diameter from tracing paper. Position over the basted seam and trace the curve of the wavy seam onto the paper. Cut along the curved line to produce two paper templates. Use the paper templates to cut one shape in gold foil, one in silver foil, and one of each shape in paper-backed fusible web. Unpick the basted seam, position the transfer paper shapes on the blocks, and iron in place. Peel off the backing paper from the metallic foil shapes and apply to the transfer paper, following the instructions for Gilding on page 39.

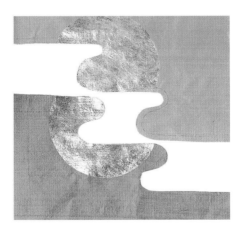

4 Photocopy the two maple leaf stencils from page 116, trace onto stencil card, and cut out the shapes with a sharp craft knife. Cut the required number of leaves from paper-backed fusible web. Using the photograph opposite as a positioning guide, apply the fusible web leaves in clusters onto the middle and right-hand panels as if they

were fluttering in the breeze. Finish with gold and silver metal leaf, following the instructions for Gilding on page 39.

5 Assemble the three panels of the screen by pinning, then basting the blocks together in the correct order. The wavy line of the upper blocks should overlap the wavy line of the lower blocks by 6 mm (¼ in) throughout. Machine embroider the blocks using a zigzag stitch in gold thread.

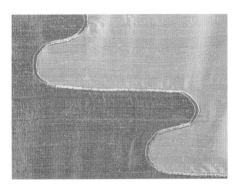

6 Photocopy the pinebark template from page 117, enlarging it so that it is 25 cm (10 in) in width. Use the template to draw three pinebark shapes onto cream raw silk. Photocopy the crane template from page 114, trace the shape onto stencil card and cut out the motif. Position the stencil centrally on the pinebark shapes and print the cranes in your chosen colors (see page 38). We used ultramarine and deep turquoise for the crane's wings and body and ocher yellow for the legs and beak. Let it dry before cutting out the stenciled pinebark shapes.

7 Draw three circles 18 cm (7 in) in diameter onto cream raw silk. Photocopy the maple branch template from page 116, trace the shape onto stencil card and cut out the motif. Position the stencil centrally on the circles of silk and print the maple branch and leaves in your chosen colors (see page 38). We chose burnt orange, created by mixing red and orange with a small amount of black, for the leaves, and brown, created by mixing ocher with green, for the branch. Let it dry before cutting out the circles of stenciled silk.

8 Back each of the stenciled silk shapes with paper-backed fusible web. Position the shapes on the panels of the screen, using the photograph opposite as a positioning guide, and iron in place. Machine embroider the raw edges using zigzag stitch in gold thread. The panels are now ready for mounting on the screen.

Noble Medallion Throw

THIS INTRICATE DESIGN WAS INSPIRED *by an eighteenth-century kimono used by actors of the No theater. The "noble" medallion shapes are indicative of a male character and would have been woven into the original garments.*

FABRICS

Background fabrics: upholstery cotton brocades and damasks in three colors – golden yellow, rusty red, and pale blue

Patchwork blocks and medallions: print fabrics in mixed fibers to complement the background fabrics – to include brocaded evening-wear fabrics in silks and satins and necktie fabrics in rich colors

Please refer to the Order of Work for specific piece sizes

MEDALLIONS

Cloud *(kumo)*

Snowflake *(yukiwa)*

Comma circle *(tomoe)*

Medallions
The cloud and the snowflake denote the onset of fall, while the comma circle and decorative Buddhist gong are chosen for their strong designs.

Gong *(choban)*

BLOCKS

ORDER OF WORK

LEFT: **Blocks**

You will need 30 blocks in total: 15 patchwork blocks and 15 appliquéd medallion blocks. Finished size of each block = 30 cm (12 in).

1 Cut 15 squares, five from each of the background fabrics, making them 30 cm (12 in) square plus 1 cm (⅜ in) seam allowances.

2 Photocopy the chosen medallions on pages 118–24, enlarging them so they are 23 cm (9 in) in diameter. Transfer the designs onto stencil card and cut out. Draw around the templates onto print brocades to contrast with the background squares cut in step 1. You will need four clouds, four comma circles, four gongs, and three snowflakes. Back with paper-backed fusible web and cut out the shapes. Fuse to a background square of the appropriate color.

3 Machine appliqué the medallions to their background squares using zigzag stitch in monofilament.

4 Photocopy the sharkstooth template on page 104 for blocks No. 1, 3, 5, 27, and 29. For each block, cut 14 triangles from background fabrics and 14 triangles from print silks, including the seam allowance marked on the template. Make five blocks by joining the triangles in the correct order (see page 26). Trim the sides with a rotary cutter to form 30 cm (12 in) blocks, plus 1 cm (⅜ in) seams.

5 The pinwheel blocks (No.7 and 9) are cut from 15 cm (6 in) squares [plus 1 cm (⅜ in) seams], which are cut once across the diagonal to make two triangles. For each block, you will need eight squares of background fabric and two squares each of four print silks. Make the blocks, alternating the colors as shown (see page 28).

6 The checkerboard blocks (No. 11, 13, and 15) are cut from 7 cm (2 ¾ in) squares plus 1 cm (⅜ in) seams. For each block, cut eight square patches from background fabric and eight from print silks. Join the patches together in pairs, combining a background fabric patch with a print fabric patch. Then join the pairs in the correct order to complete the block.

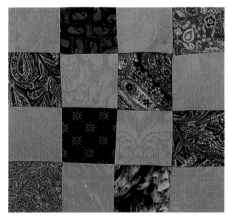

7 The bow-tie blocks (No. 17 and 19) are cut from nine 10 cm (4 in) squares [plus 1 cm (⅜ in) seams] of background fabric and

silks, which are cut twice across the diagonal to make four equal triangles. Join the bow-tie triangles (see page 28), alternating the colors as shown below.

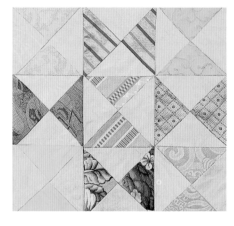

8 For the diamond blocks (No. 21, 23, and 25), cut sixteen 10 cm (4 in) squares from background fabric and nine from print silks, plus 1 cm (⅜ in) seams. Join the patches in the correct order, set on point, then trim the sides to form a 30 cm (12 in) block, plus 1 cm (⅜ in) seams.

9 When all the blocks are complete, arrange them in order on a flat surface, ready for stitching together. First join the blocks in horizontal rows (starting with blocks 1–5). Press the seams to one side on the back. When the horizontal rows are complete, join them in the correct order to complete the block, matching seams carefully. The patchwork is now ready to back and finish as you wish.

Pinebark Throw

A ZIGZAG PATTERN *is created using the distinctive pinebark lozenge shape (matsukawa-bishi), which is thought to resemble the scale of a pine cone. The strong, contrasting shades of red and green with accents of blue and gold are redolent of fall days.*

APPLIQUÉD SHAPES

You will need two pinebark strips, 36 large pinebark lozenges, and 19 small pinebark lozenges

Finished size of throw = 250 x 150 cm (96 x 60 in)

FABRICS

Background fabric and pinebark strips: plain silk in two colors — we used deep red and pale green

Pinebark lozenges: print and solid (plain) fabrics in light and dark tones, with gold as neutral

Please refer to the Order of Work for specific piece sizes

ABOVE: **Appliquéd shapes**

Two large rectangles of solid (plain) silk (not shown) — one deep red and one a paler tone of green — are joined together at the center to form a basis for the appliquéd shapes. The individual pinebark patches are arranged in horizontal rows at 5 cm (2 in) intervals, which gives a subsidiary pattern where areas of background fabric show through. (Small lozenges are appliquéd inside others for added interest.) To finish, two pinebark strips in contrasting background fabrics are appliquéd to opposite ends of the throw.

ORDER OF WORK

1 Cut two large rectangles 125 x 75 cm (48 x 30 in) plus 5 mm (¼ in) seams, one from each of your background fabrics. Seam the fabrics together along their shortest edges.

2 Photocopy the lozenge templates from page 110, enlarging them so that the widest point of the large lozenge measures 30 cm (12 in) and the small lozenge measures 14 cm (5½ in). Cut 36 large lozenge patches and 19 small lozenge patches from solid (plain) and print silk. Back each shape with paper-backed fusible web.

3 Arrange the patches in rows on the background fabric, moving them around until you are happy with the colors. Position the two rows of pinebark patches in the center so that they meet exactly in the middle. The remaining horizontal rows are spaced at 5 cm (2 in) intervals so that the background fabric shows through, giving the zigzag effect.

4 Remove the backing papers and press the shapes in position. Zigzag around the raw edges with monofilament, then trim the sides even with the background fabric.

5 Trace the pinebark strip template from page 110, and repeat so that it is four times the length. Enlarge it so that the widest point measures 120 cm (48 in). Use to cut two pieces of background fabric, one in each color. Back with iron-on transfer paper, then position on the throw. Press lightly in place before zigzag stitching in monofilament.

WINTER

IN JAPAN each season is very different and has its own unique quality and atmosphere. The snowy landscapes of winter are recorded in all their cold, ethereal beauty onto all types of surfaces, so that they can then be brought out and used in the hot, humid days of summer as a refreshing reminder of coolness. The icy snow crystals sparkling in gold and silver on the "shimmering wall hanging" could be put to the same purpose.

Plants that retain their leaves and flowers in the winter are regarded as noble or brave since they stay with us throughout the dead time of the year. Pine, bamboo, and plum are called "the three friends of winter," and are among the most popular decorative motifs.

The austerity that winter evokes is often reflected in the use of simple rustic materials for fabrics; cottons, linens, and hemp are woven in neutral-colored stripes and checks called *koshi*, or printed with small-scale patterns called *komon* designs.

Shimmering Wallhanging

GLISTENING SILKS AND METALLIC *fabrics in cool grays and icy silvers are combined to create a striking wallhanging. The gilded medallions are all symbols of winter in Japan. They include a bamboo laden with snow, a plum blossom, a snowflake, and a cloud.*

FABRICS

Background fabric: dark metallic fabric for the medallion triangle

Pieced triangles: metallic fabric in four pale colors and silk dupion in four pale colors, for example, gold, ocher, silver, and gray

Medallions: gold and silver metallic leaf

Please refer to the Order of Work for specific piece sizes

BLOCKS

You will need one medallion triangle, six pieced triangles, and three solid (plain) triangles. Finished size of hanging = 90 cm (35½ in) square.

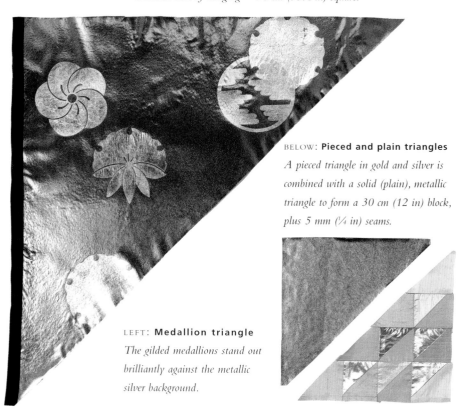

BELOW: **Pieced and plain triangles**
A pieced triangle in gold and silver is combined with a solid (plain), metallic triangle to form a 30 cm (12 in) block, plus 5 mm (¼ in) seams.

LEFT: **Medallion triangle**
The gilded medallions stand out brilliantly against the metallic silver background.

ORDER OF WORK

1 Cut the large medallion triangle from background fabric, making it 90 cm (35½ in) across at the base and side, plus 5 mm (¼ in) seam allowances.

2 Choose from the templates on pages 118–24 to cut five medallions 20 cm (8 in) in diameter from iron-on transfer paper. Gild the medallions to the background triangle (see page 39), using the photograph as a positioning guide.

3 The lower triangle is made of six pieced triangles. For each pieced triangle, cut 18 squares, 7.5 cm (3 in) plus 5 mm (¼ in) seams, in metallic fabrics and 30 in silks. Cut each square across the diagonal to form equal triangles. Using 5 mm (¼ in) seam allowances, make 36 triangle patches by joining a metallic triangle to a silk triangle to form a square. Make six pieced triangles, using six triangle patches and four solid (plain) triangles for each.

4 Cut three solid (plain) triangles the same size as the finished pieced triangles from metallic fabric. Join a pieced triangle to a plain triangle to form a block.

5 Make the lower triangle by stitching the pieced triangles and triangle blocks together in the order shown. Join the finished lower triangle to the gilded medallion triangle to complete the patchwork. The hanging is now ready to back and finish as you wish.

Tortoiseshell Cushion

THE FAMILIAR HEXAGON PATCH *shown here in its double and single form is known as "kikko" in Japan, meaning tortoiseshell. Individual diamond shapes make up the lower half of the cushion to give the pinebark pattern.*

FABRICS

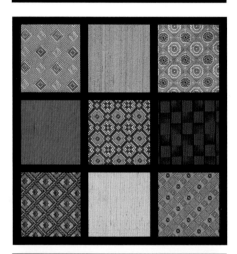

Tortoiseshell block: small-scale woven print brocades, necktie fabrics, and silk dupion in three solid (plain) colors

Solid (plain) strip and pinebark block: silk dupions in solid (plain) and two-tone colors, necktie fabric, and textured brocade

Please refer to the Order of Work for specific piece sizes

BLOCKS

You will need one tortoiseshell block, one solid (plain) strip, and one pinebark block.
Finished size of cushion = 43 cm (17 in) square.

RIGHT: **Tortoiseshell block**
The tortoiseshell block is composed of double and single hexagons in complementary shades of blue, gold, and purple, which are joined by hand.

RIGHT: **Silk strip**
The two styles of patchwork block are stitched onto a strip of solid (plain) silk.

RIGHT: **Pinebark block**
The pinebark block is made of small hand-stitched diamond shapes in solid (plain) and print textured silks.

ORDER OF WORK

1 Photocopy the hexagon and quadrilateral templates for the tortoiseshell block from page 105 and cut out the required number of patches and backing papers. Join the shapes by hand (see page 21), then remove all but the bottom row of backing papers. Trim the top and sides to form a block measuring 45 x 23 cm (18 x 9 in).

2 Photocopy the diamond templates for the pinebark block from page 105 and cut the required number of patches from solid (plain) and print silks. Join the patches by hand in groups of four, then join the groups together to form a block (see page 23). Remove all but the top row of backing papers, then trim the base and sides.

3 Cut a silk rectangle 45 x 10 cm (18 x 4 in) plus 5 mm (¼ in) for seams, to fit between the pinebark and tortoiseshell blocks.

4 Pin and baste the tortoiseshell and pinebark blocks to the silk strip so that the points of the diamonds meet the points of the hexagons in the middle. Hand stitch in place.

Mist and Snow Bedcover

THIS COVER IS BASED ON *"yogi" nightwear, or extra-large padded kimonos that were traditionally used as bed covers in rural Japan. Originally the yogi was made from recycled kimonos, but it evolved into a wedding gift that parents would present to their daughters.*

FABRICS

White cotton for dyeing

Background fabrics: striped cotton and printed kimono fabric (we used a small floral print)

Kimono patchwork and medallions: assorted fabric scraps – to include solid (plain) deep blues, floral prints in various sizes, and small geometric prints

Please refer to the Order of Work for specific piece sizes

MEDALLIONS

ABOVE: **Snowflakes**

The five snowflake medallions (yukiwa) are cut from large floral fabrics to stand out against the various background prints. A template is given on page 124.

BLOCKS

ORDER OF WORK

LEFT: **Blocks**

Measurements are given for a single bed cover 163 x 122 cm (64 x 48 in). The finished size of each block is 30 cm (12 in) square plus 5 mm (¼ in) seams. For a double bed, increase the size of each block to 46 cm (18 in) square plus 5 mm (¼ in) seams.

1 Use the template on page 124 to cut five snowflake motifs 20 cm (8 in) in diameter from large print fabrics, using light, medium, and dark prints to stand out against the various background fabrics. Back each shape with iron-on transfer paper.

2 Cut five 30 cm (12 in) squares [plus 5 mm (¼ in) seams] from white cotton and dye them in deep blue using the dip-dyeing process on page 37 for blocks 5, 6, 7, and 8. Leave one of the squares in the dye bath for the duration of the dyeing, to be used for the "collar" of the kimono (blocks 2 and 3).

3 For blocks 22 and 23, cut 32 square patches in solid (plain) fabric and 18 square patches in print fabrics, making them 6.5 cm (2 ⅜ in) square plus 5 mm (¼ in) seams. For each block, join 16 solid (plain) squares and nine print squares by machine, alternating the colors as shown to create a checkerboard effect. Set the blocks on point and trim the sides with a rotary cutter to form a 30 cm (12 in) block plus 5 mm (¼ in) seams.

4 Blocks 18 and 19 are assembled in the same way as blocks 22 and 23. Cut the required number of 10 cm (4 in) squares plus 5 mm (¼ in) seams from solid (plain) fabric, print fabric, and kimono ground fabric. You will need 25 squares in total for each block. Join the squares and trim to form a 30 cm (12 in) block plus 5 mm (¼ in) seams.

5 Cut six 30 cm (12 in) squares and two 15 x 30 cm (6 x 12 in) rectangles [plus 5 mm (¼ in) seams] from kimono ground fabric. Trace the appliqué cloud template for pieces 9, 10, 11, 12, 13, 14, and 15 from page 119. Cut out the shapes from white cotton and position on the background squares and rectangles. Machine appliqué using satin stitch in matching thread.

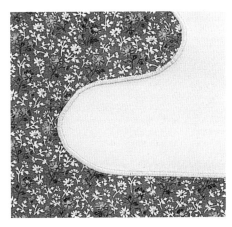

6 For blocks 17, 20, 21, and 24, cut sixteen 15 cm (6 in) squares plus 5 mm (¼ in) seam allowance, from striped fabric and join together to make four four-patch blocks.

7 For blocks 13 and 16, cut four 15 cm (6 in) squares [plus 5 mm (¼ in) seams] from striped fabric and join in pairs. Press seams to one side, then join to a kimono fabric rectangle cut in step 5.

8 For blocks 1 and 4, cut four 12 x 15 cm (4½ x 6 in) patches [plus 5 mm (¼ in) seams] from striped fabric and stitch in pairs.

9 For blocks 2 and 3, cut four 12 x 15 cm (4½ x 6 in) patches [plus 5 mm (¼ in) seams] from striped fabric and one 25 cm (10 in) square [plus 5 mm (¼ in) seams] from dyed cotton (see step 2). Cut the dyed square in half across the diagonal to form two triangles. With right sides together, stitch a dyed triangle to a striped rectangle. Join to another striped rectangle to form a block.

10 When all the separate blocks are complete, machine stitch them together in rows, starting with blocks 1–4, to form five horizontal strips of patchwork. Press all the seams to one side. Now join the strips together, matching seams carefully.

11 Position the snowflakes and appliqué using zigzag stitch in monofilament. The bed cover is now ready for backing.

Three Friends Screen

THE BAMBOO, PINE, AND PLUM TREE *are described as the "three friends of winter" in*

Japan because they all provide color early in the year. The images are often featured together

in Japanese design, and here they are placed against a background of crazy patchwork.

FABRICS

Background fabric: solid (plain) linen in a neutral color

Crazy fabrics: a selection of prints and woven brocades in cotton and linen (these can be pieced together to create a series of patchwork blocks)

Please refer to the Order of Work for specific piece sizes

MEDALLIONS

You will need one appliquéd bamboo medallion, one appliquéd plum blossom medallion, and one appliquéd pine tree medallion.

RIGHT: **Appliquéd medallions**
The three appliquéd medallions are arranged on a background of crazy patchwork. Notice how the strongest colored cottons are used for the appliquéd motifs to make them stand out against the random patchwork panels. You can give the medallions extra impact by embroidering them in matching or contrasting colored thread.

Bamboo (page 118)

Pine tree (page 122)

Plum blossom (page 12

ORDER OF WORK

1 Cut three pieces of background fabric the same size as the panels, adding 15 cm (6 in) to the length and 5cm (2 in) to each side to allow for mounting.

2 Cut the "crazy" fabrics into random shapes and mount on paper-backed fusible web. We included several patchwork

blocks in the design, which were left over from other projects. Arrange the fabric patches on the three panels, following the instructions for Crazy Patchwork on page 32. Notice how some of the background fabric is left exposed to give space and unity to the design. Secure the patches using a small zigzag stitch in a contrasting color.

3 Photocopy the three medallion templates from the pages shown above and cut one of each shape in your chosen fabrics. Cut three circles, 30 cm (12 in) in diameter, from background fabric. Appliqué the medallions onto the circles, using a small zigzag stitch in matching thread (see page 41). Position the appliquéd circles on the screen and zigzag in place.

templates and motifs

Patchwork Templates

(All shown at 100% size unless otherwise stated)

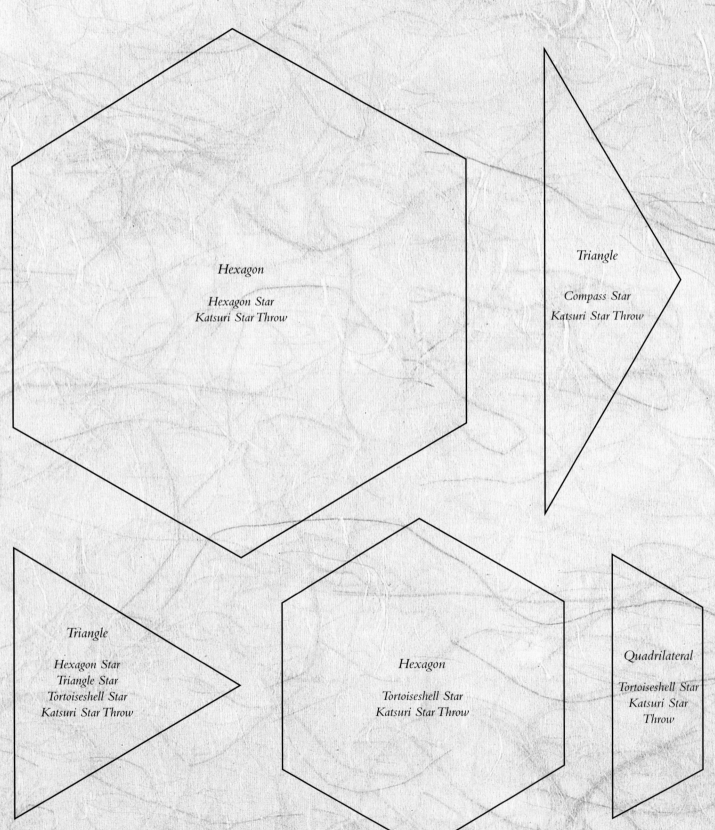

Hexagon

Hexagon Star
Katsuri Star Throw

Triangle

Compass Star
Katsuri Star Throw

Triangle

Hexagon Star
Triangle Star
Tortoiseshell Star
Katsuri Star Throw

Hexagon

Tortoiseshell Star
Katsuri Star Throw

Quadrilateral

Tortoiseshell Star
Katsuri Star
Throw

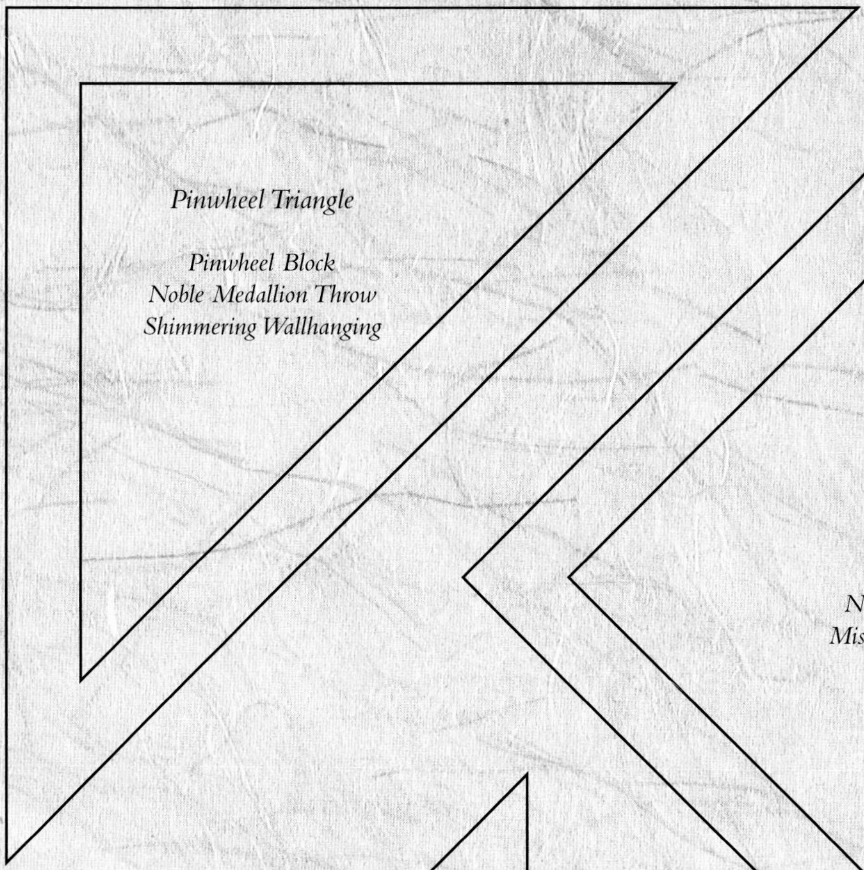

Pinwheel Triangle

Pinwheel Block
Noble Medallion Throw
Shimmering Wallhanging

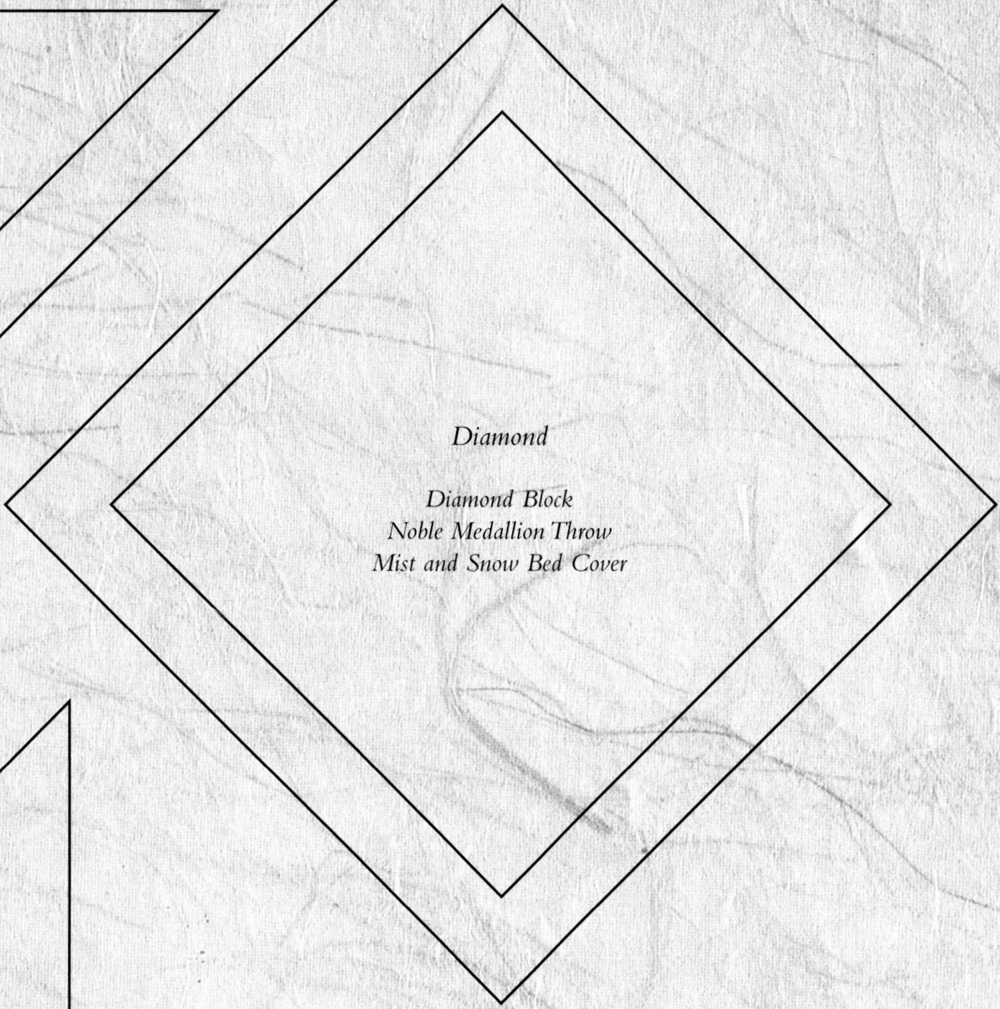

Diamond

Diamond Block
Noble Medallion Throw
Mist and Snow Bed Cover

Bow-tie Triangle

Bow-tie Block
Noble Medallion Throw

Checkerboard Square

Checkerboard Block
Noble Medallion Throw
Three Friends Screen
Spring Fan Screen

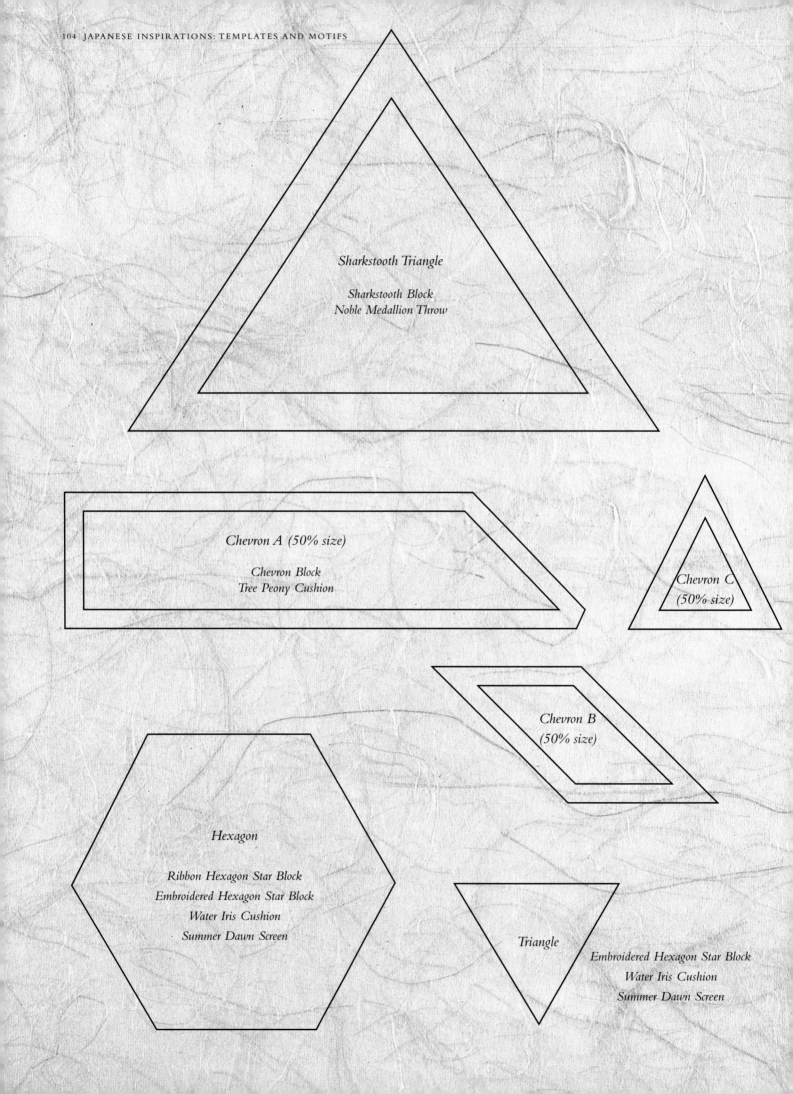

Sharkstooth Triangle

Sharkstooth Block
Noble Medallion Throw

Chevron A (50% size)

Chevron Block
Tree Peony Cushion

Chevron C
(50% size)

Chevron B
(50% size)

Hexagon

Ribbon Hexagon Star Block
Embroidered Hexagon Star Block
Water Iris Cushion
Summer Dawn Screen

Triangle

Embroidered Hexagon Star Block
Water Iris Cushion
Summer Dawn Screen

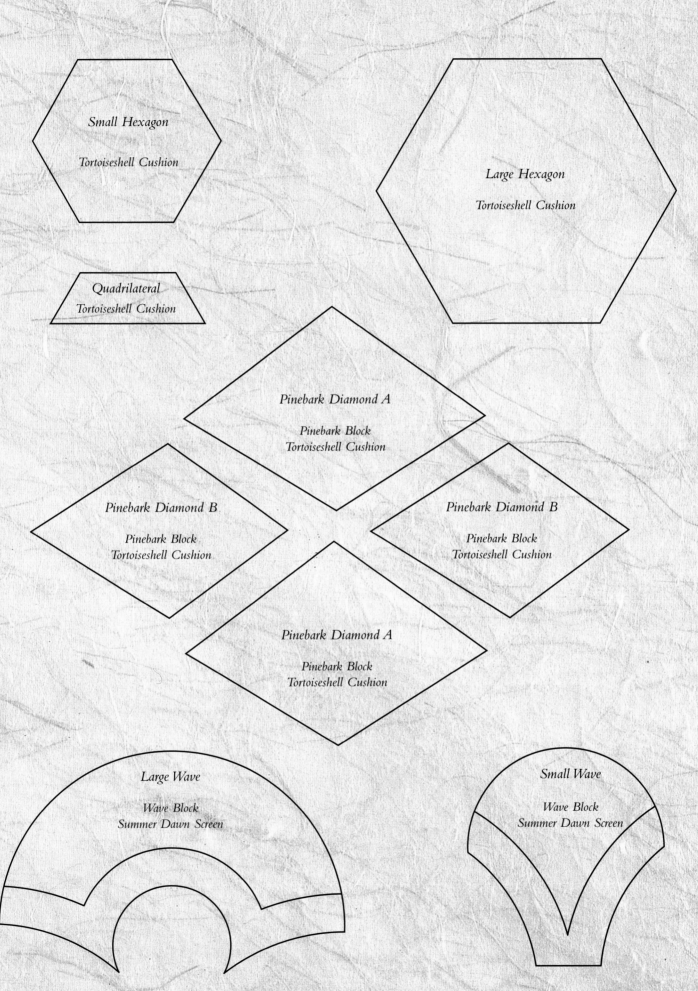

Small Hexagon

Tortoiseshell Cushion

Large Hexagon

Tortoiseshell Cushion

Quadrilateral
Tortoiseshell Cushion

Pinebark Diamond A

Pinebark Block
Tortoiseshell Cushion

Pinebark Diamond B

Pinebark Block
Tortoiseshell Cushion

Pinebark Diamond B

Pinebark Block
Tortoiseshell Cushion

Pinebark Diamond A

Pinebark Block
Tortoiseshell Cushion

Large Wave

Wave Block
Summer Dawn Screen

Small Wave

Wave Block
Summer Dawn Screen

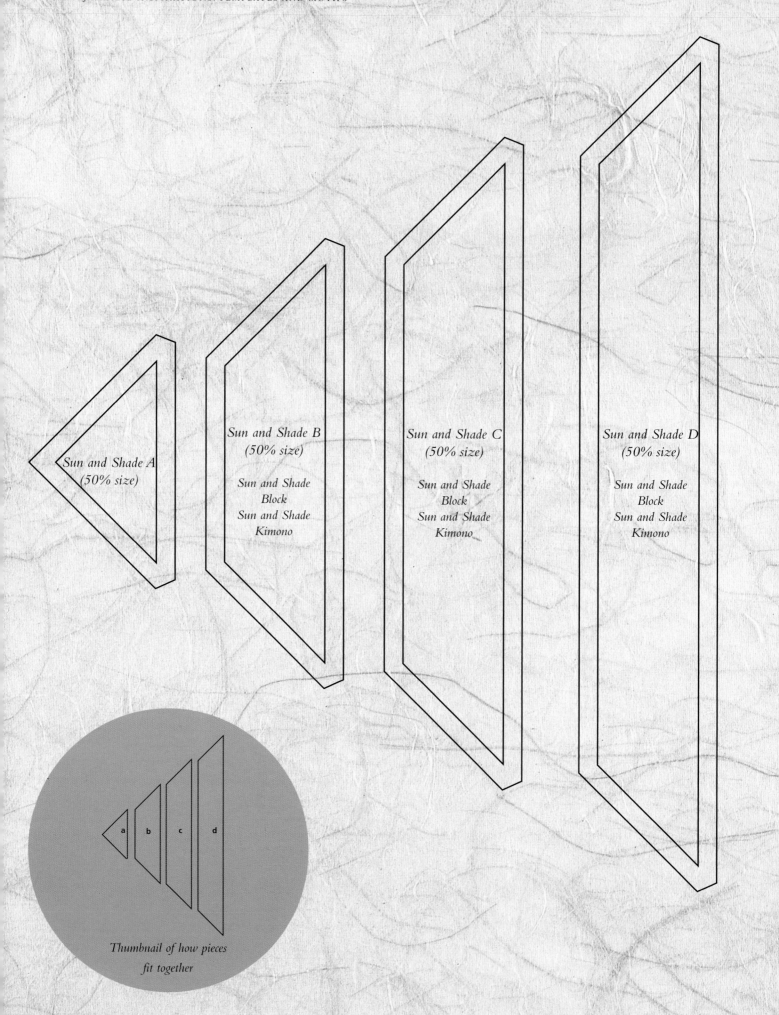

Sun and Shade A
(50% size)

Sun and Shade B
(50% size)

Sun and Shade
Block
Sun and Shade
Kimono

Sun and Shade C
(50% size)

Sun and Shade
Block
Sun and Shade
Kimono

Sun and Shade D
(50% size)

Sun and Shade
Block
Sun and Shade
Kimono

Thumbnail of how pieces
fit together

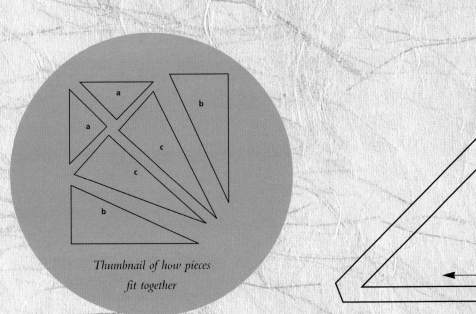

*Thumbnail of how pieces
fit together*

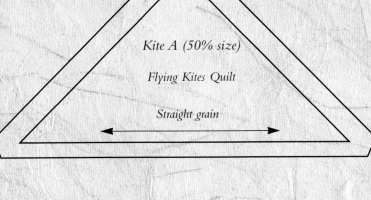

Kite A (50% size)

Flying Kites Quilt

Straight grain

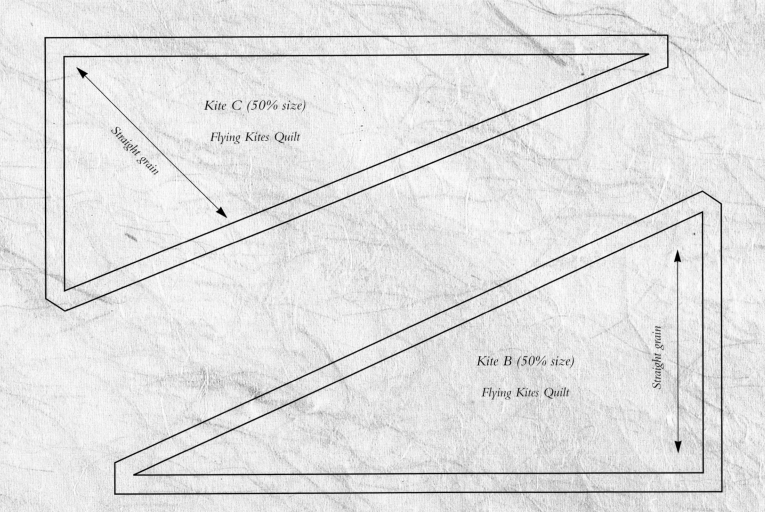

Kite C (50% size)

Flying Kites Quilt

Straight grain

Kite B (50% size)

Flying Kites Quilt

Straight grain

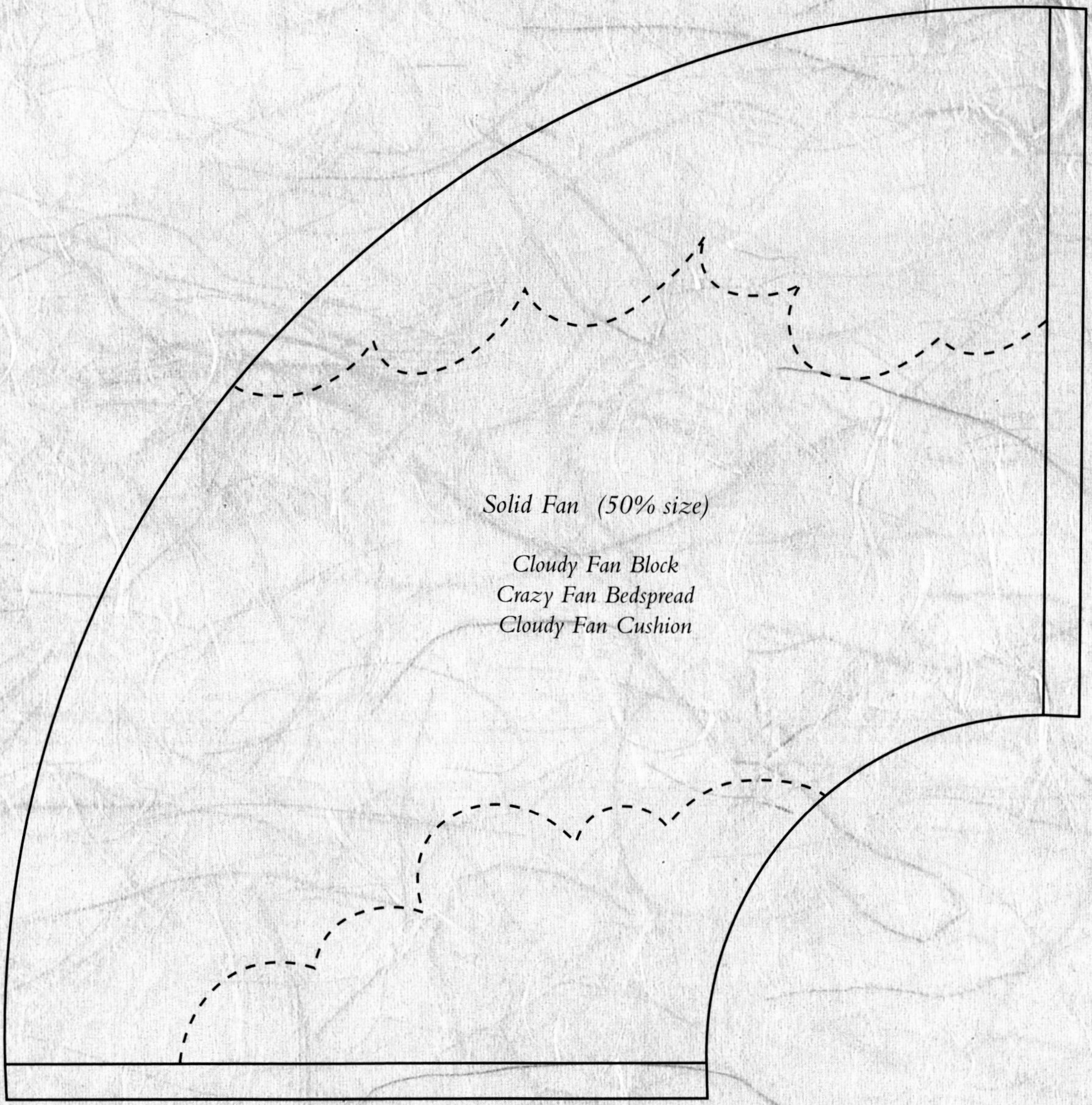

Solid Fan (50% size)

Cloudy Fan Block
Crazy Fan Bedspread
Cloudy Fan Cushion

Cloud Shape A (50% size)

Cloudy Fan Block
Crazy Fan Bedspread
Cloudy Fan Cushion

Triangle

Cloudy Fan Cushion

*Fan Blade
(50% size)*

*Crazy Fan
Bedspread*

Square

Cloudy Fan Cushion

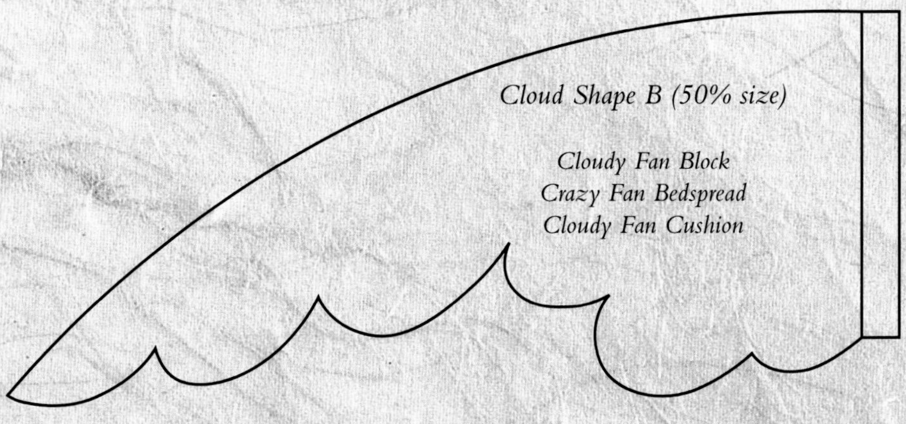

Cloud Shape B (50% size)

*Cloudy Fan Block
Crazy Fan Bedspread
Cloudy Fan Cushion*

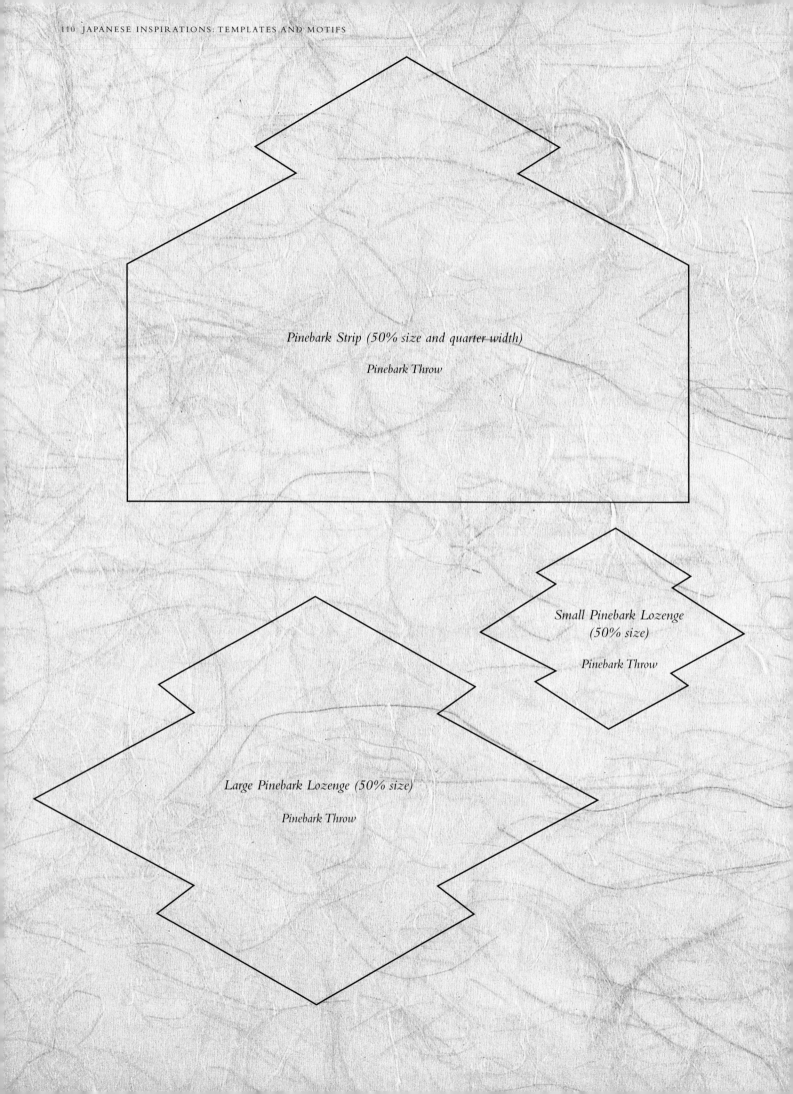

Pinebark Strip (50% size and quarter width)

Pinebark Throw

*Small Pinebark Lozenge
(50% size)*

Pinebark Throw

Large Pinebark Lozenge (50% size)

Pinebark Throw

Indigo Kimono C
(50% size)

Indigo Kimono Quilt

Thumbnail of how pieces
fit together

Indigo
Kimono E
(50% size)

Indigo Kimono B
(50% size)

Indigo Kimono Quilt

Indigo
Kimono F
(50% size)

Indigo Kimono
Quilt

Indigo Kimono A
(50% size)

Indigo Kimono Quilt

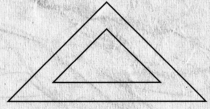

Indigo Kimono D
(50% size)

Indigo Kimono Quilt

Decorative Motifs

(All shown at 100% size unless otherwise stated)

Iris

Wisteria

Peony

Cherry Blossom

Crane

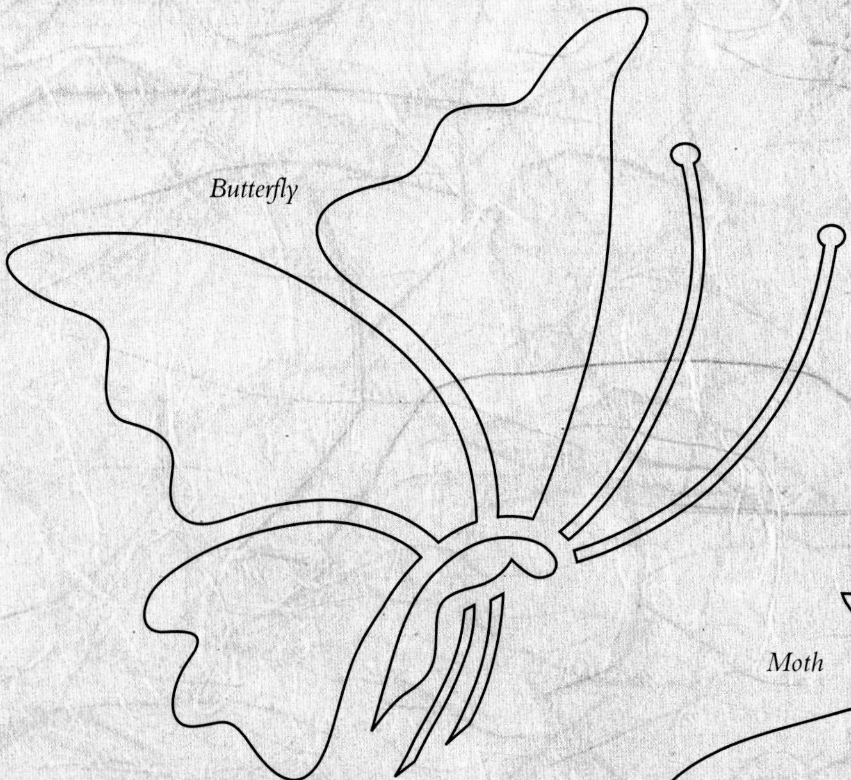

Moth

Butterfly

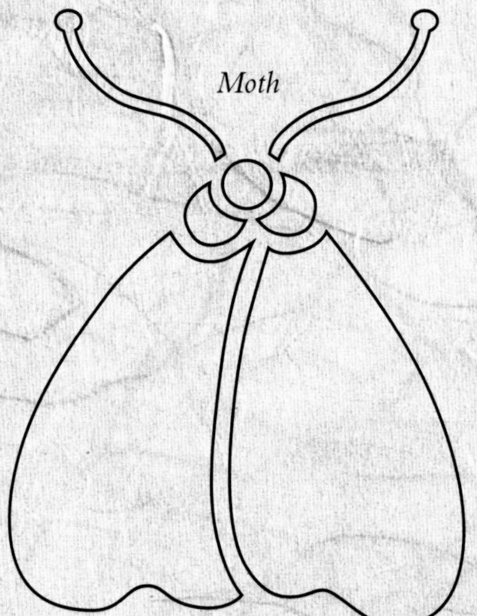

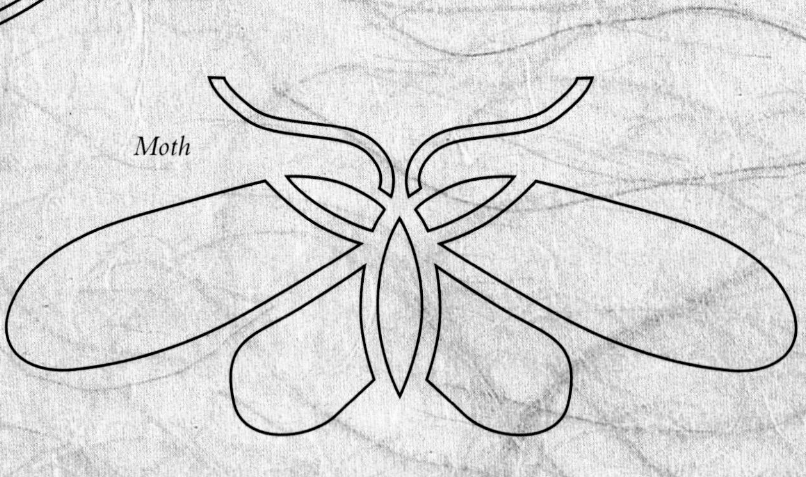

Moth

Dragonfly

Diving House Martin

Soaring House Martin

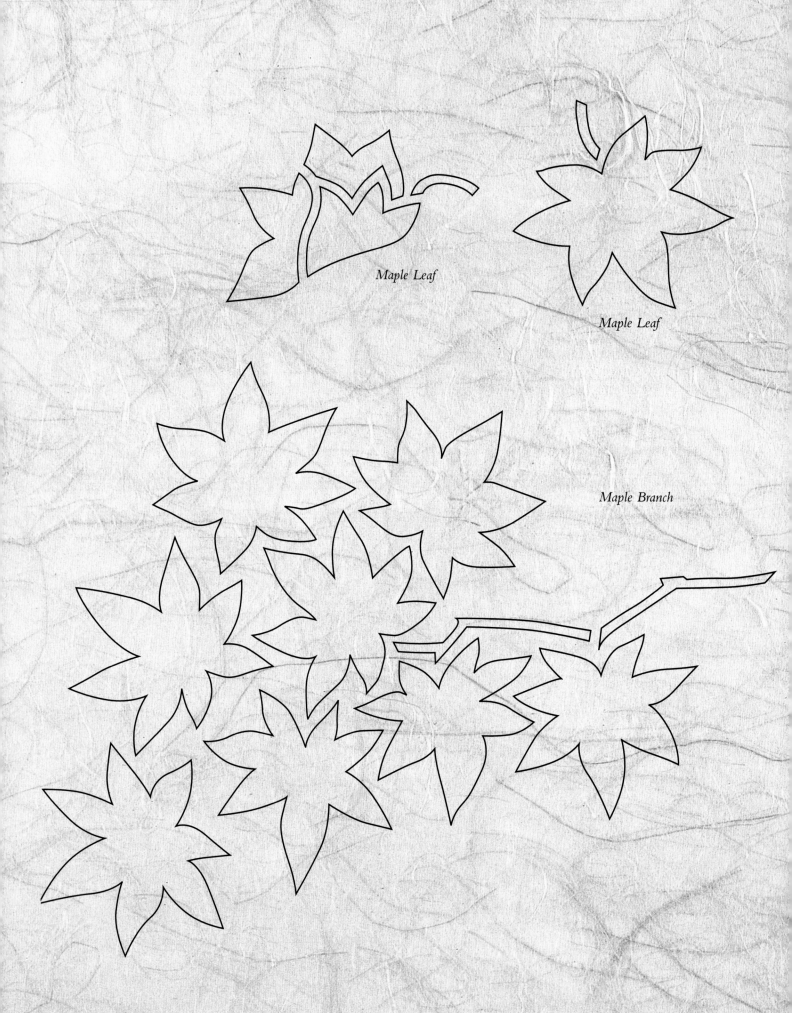

Maple Leaf

Maple Leaf

Maple Branch

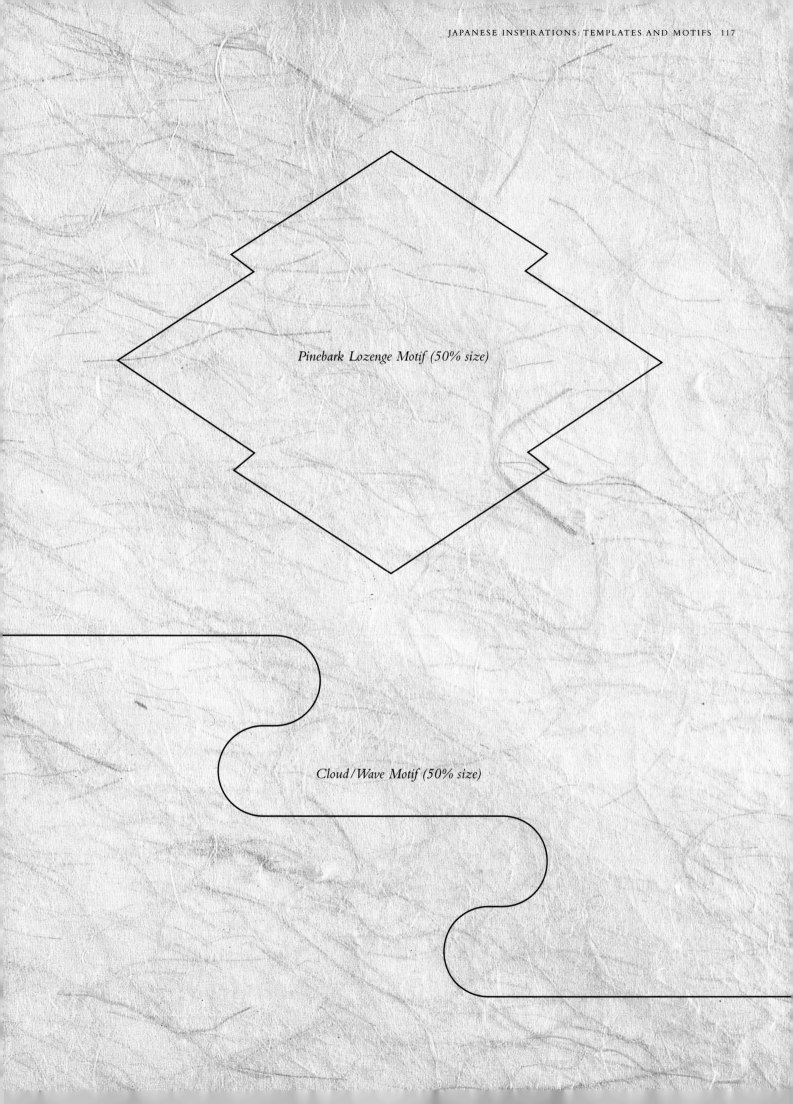

Pinebark Lozenge Motif (50% size)

Cloud/Wave Motif (50% size)

Bamboo and Snowflake

Clouds

Commas

Gong

Pine

Plum Blossom

Snowflake

Large and Small Fans (50% size)

index

bibliography

Kato, Amy, *Blue and White Japan*, Charles E. Tuttle Co., Inc, Rutland, Vermont, 1996.

Kennedy, Alan, *Japanese Costume, History and Tradition*, Editions Adam Biro, Paris, 1990.

Lee, Sherman E., *The Genius of Japanese Design*, Kodansha International, Tokyo, New York, San Francisco.

Nakano, Eisho, and Stephan, Barbara B., *JapaneseStencil Dyeing*, Weatherhill, Tokyo and New York, 1982.

Noma, Serioku, *Japanese Costume and Textile Arts*, Heibonsha, Tokyo and Weatherhill, New York, 1974.

Seri, Nihon, and Sentam, Ishom, *Textile Designs of Japan: Free Style Designs*, Vol. 1, Serindia Publications, Kyoto, 1980.

Seri, Nihon, and Sentam, Ishom, *Textile Designs of Japan: Geometric Designs*, Vol. 2, Serindia Publications, Kyoto, 1980.

Stafford, Carleton L., and Bishop, Robert, *Americas Quilts and Coverlets*, Cassell and Collier Macmillan, New York, 1974.

Statler, Oliver, *All-Japan: The catalogue of everything Japanese*, Columbus Books, 1984.

acknowledgments

WORKING ON THIS BOOK has refreshed my memories and rekindled my interest in all things Japanese. I am indebted to my Japanese "family," Atsuko Morimoto and her mother Fusako Kubo, who have been so generous in sending materials that have helped to make this book a visual pleasure.

Meanwhile in England, Hilary Jagger, expert hand patchworker, Debbie Mole, inspirational art editor, and John Heseltine, laid-back photographer, worked with me with their usual mixture of irony and expertise to make up the the team responsible for the creative work within the book.

Thanks to Sarah Hoggett, Catherine Ward, and Clare Churly for their support at Collins & Brown. Friends and colleagues also helped me. Shelagh Antonovics lent me contemporary Japanese craft and design books and Yvonne Sargent donated exotic fabric scraps for the projects.

And to my brother, Colin Haigh, who unknowingly triggered my delight in all things Oriental all those years ago; thanks for all the prezzies Col.

suppliers' credits

The author would like to thank Jim Moeller at The Silver Thimble for all his support and for supplying the Au Ver a Soie silk yarns used in the embroidery motifs.

Mary and Shiro Tamakoshi at Euro Japan Links for their help in supplying the Japanese fabrics for the book.

Euro Japan Links, 32 Nant Road, Childs Hill, London, NW2 2AT. Tel: (020) 8201 9324.

The Quilt Room (mail order), Rear Carvilles, Station Road, Dorking, RH4 1XH. Tel: (01306) 877307.

To find a supplier of Au Ver a Soie threads near you, contact one of the distributors listed below for information:
U.K.: The Silver Thimble, The Old Malthouse, Clarence Street, Bath, BA1 5NS. Tel: (01225) 423 457.
U.S.A.: Access Commodities Inc, PO Box 1355, 1129 S. Virginia Street, Terrell, Texas 75160. Tel: (972) 563 3313.
Canada: As for U.S.A.
Australia: Stadia Trading Pty Ltd, Beaconsfield, NSW 2014. Tel: 9565 4666.